The
Wicca
Bible

the
wicca
bible

THE DEFINITIVE GUIDE TO
MAGIC AND THE CRAFT

Ann-Marie Gallagher

STERLING

New York / London
www.sterlingpublishing.com

Library of Congress Cataloging-in-Publication Data
Available

10   9   8   7   6

First published in Great Britain in 2005
by Godsfield Press, a division of
Octopus Publishing Group Ltd
Endeavour House, 189 Shaftesbury Avenue,
London, WC2H 8JY

Published by Sterling Publishing Co., Inc.
387 Park Avenue South, New York, NY 10016

Distributed in Canada by Sterling Publishing
c/o Canadian Manda Group, 165 Dufferin Street
Toronto, Ontario, Canada M6K 3H6

Printed in China

Sterling ISBN 13: 978-1-4027-3008-5

Contents

Introduction

Wicca is the religion and practice of witches, or "the Wise," as we are sometimes known. It has been described as the fastest-growing religion in the West, though nobody really knows how many Wiccans there are in the world. Judging by the number of internet sites and formal groups cropping up around the globe, particularly in Britain, continental Europe and the USA, it is clear that the growth of the Wiccan movement is quite phenomenal.

Perhaps this is not all that surprising. Over the last few decades, public interest in the environment, in alternative healing therapies, self-development, holistic food and medicine, social justice and, significantly, in "alternative" spiritualities and magic has developed tremendously. Wicca explores many of these concerns within an inclusive spiritual path that honors the diversity and divinity of nature and advises its followers to "harm none." If you read carefully through the different sections of this book, participate in the activities it guides

Wicca is a nature religion. Wiccans see the divine in nature, both within us and around us.

you through and learn more about practising Wicca, you will begin to understand exactly why Wicca, sometimes called "the Craft," has grown in popularity and why, in the twenty-first century, people are declaring themselves "Wicce" or "Witches."

Because Wicca is a religion that does not have a doctrine or a set central priesthood, sacred texts or sets of rules, the responsibility for learning and growing within the chosen spiritual path is placed upon the individual. Even though there are some established traditions within the Wiccan community, many have grown out of exploration and continue to evolve as Wiccans learn which practices and points of understanding are essential, and which are more flexible.

Practicing spirituality outside the limiting strictures of a set "organized" religion can be a very liberating experience, but it can also be extraordinarily demanding on the individual, requiring considerable resourcefulness. Some novices will be lucky enough to have friends or family who are Wiccan, and thus have good sources of advice only a phone call away. The majority of us, though, start out with an interest that we want to explore privately before joining a group or sounding out others for counsel.

The main purpose of this book is to provide a detailed resource of information—and inspiration—both for those who are encountering Wicca for the first time and for those who are already treading that path. All the information and guidance you need on the key aspects of Wicca as a philosophy, a spiritual path and a magical tradition are explored. Knowledge of these key aspects will help direct you through the exciting territory that is Wiccan spirituality and practice, and help you develop your own understanding and sense of the spiritual on your travels.

Wiccans recognize the value of continuing to develop our understanding and practices; just as the world constantly changes around us, so we, too, must acknowledge the need to grow and extend our knowledge and skills. There is scope within the book for those who already have some knowledge of the ways of the Wise to develop that further, or to revisit their understanding of different aspects of Wicca.

Welcome, then, to Wicca as it is practiced by the Wise, with its regional variations and in its many diverse flavors all over the globe. Welcome also to a tradition that casts a look over its shoulder into the past to find a spiritual affinity with our ancestors, and looks forward to the future for new ways of living with each other, with the rhythms of the Earth and nature. And if you are setting your foot on the path of the Wise, then as the Wicce say, Blessed Be.

The chalice is a symbol of healing, communion and initiation.

Wicca works with the rhythms and tides of nature.

how to use the book

For the beginner, the best and most effective way to use this book when reading it for the first time is to work through it in order, trying the various exercises as you proceed. It is also best, if you are new to Wicca, to read through What is Wicca? (see pages 14–47), which will give you a good foundation for what follows.

Each section has an introductory segment with background and guidance to the information and exercises that follow. It is important to read the introductions carefully as they often define and explain terminology and provide information vital to the practical work in the sections. For example, the introduction to Visualization (see pages 132–139) offers a beginner's guide to visualization, including practical guidance on how to prepare physically and how to create the sacred space in which to work. Ignoring this advice may adversely affect your progress through the exercises and lead to frustration. In particular, if you are tempted to dip into the spells in Magic (see pages 242–277), it is vital that you read the introduction that explains the principles, laws and ethics to which practicing magicians adhere.

For the more experienced, it is still a good idea to read through What is Wicca? (see pages 14–47) so that you are clear about the basis on which this book is written. Beyond that, your experience will enable you to dip in and out of the text at will for information, ideas and inspiration for your solo or coven work. However, remember to read the introduction to any section you intend to dip into as this will remind you of

Preparation is important. This witch censes the sacred space prior to ritual.

11

Traditionally, handfasting lasts for a year and a day.

the basic disciplines and reasoning behind the way the section is presented. If you are a teacher, you may find good resource material on the passage of the Wiccan year and its eight Sabbats (see pages 48–73) as well as some suggested activities for attuning to the five sacred Elements (see pages 74–89).

The beginner and experienced practitioner alike will find a wealth of information within Paths and traditions (see pages 90–101) which is based on experience of and research into Wiccan beliefs and practices. You will find explanations or reminders of the importance to witches of the circle and sacred space, as well as directions on how to create that space. Similarly, you will be able to access magical guidelines that explore the premise upon which spell-work is built, as well as ways to develop yourself magically. There is also guidance on the timing of spells and rituals, including moon and sun cycles, days of the week, planetary hours and astrological information (see pages 210–217), as well as a useful glossary of the main gods and goddesses honored in the Wiccan tradition, complete with totem and symbol information (see pages 108–131). Developing skills and knowledge (see pages 278–363) is particularly rich in quick-reference information, and includes guides to dream symbolism (see pages 284–289), the Qabalah (see pages 302–307), Wiccan symbols (see pages 314–319), colors (see pages 320–323) and common magical herbs, oils and incenses (see pages 324–343) and the Runes (see pages 350–357).

For those interested in divination, there is guidance within the above section to astrology, the Tarot and "scrying" (the art of divination by looking into mirrors, crystal balls or water). These aspects of divination are indicative rather than comprehensive, and are intended as a starting point for those working within the Craft and its traditions.

In addition, you will find practical advice on the everyday business of Wicca, including how to put together an altar, acquire and consecrate magical tools, cast a circle (sacred space), prepare for initiation, choose a magical name, work safely with fire and cook for a coven meeting.

Whether you are new to Wicca or an experienced practitioner, this book should help you build and enhance your knowledge and skills in the Craft. Bright blessings on the path!

An athame and wand can both be used to direct energy.

what is wicca?

Wicca—what it is and what it is not

These days, Wicca refers to a set of practices, beliefs and traditions associated with people who call themselves witches. Witches call themselves Wicca ("wise" in Anglo-Saxon), not because they think they know more or better than anyone else, but because historically this expression referred to people who worked with nature and magic. In Wicca, wisdom is an aspiration rather than a starting point, and learning is an ongoing process. This requires those who wish to join the ranks of "the Wise" to acknowledge and accept the constant processes of change and development both within us and within the world around us. This adaptability is appropriate as, apparently, a secondary meaning of the word *Wicca* was "bendy" or "wiggly."

On the subject of meaning, there is a distinction between the way that the word *Wicca* is interpreted in Britain and its customary usage in North America. References to Wicca in Britain have traditionally alluded to a specific initiatory system of witchcraft as practiced within covens that follow either Alexandrian or Gardnerian witchcraft, or a synthesis of both sometimes called British or English traditional

A broomstick is used to prepare sacred space.

witchcraft (for descriptions of different traditions of Wicca see pages 90–101). This definition of the term excludes solo practitioners of the craft, and those groups who are rather more eclectic in their practices.

In North America, the term is used in a more inclusive way—it refers to all those who number themselves among "the Wise," whether solo practitioners or members of groups who fall outside the Alexandrian/Gardnerian definition. In this book, I take this latter sense in which the term is applied—and I am happy to report that references to Wicca in Britain are shifting slowly toward this more all-embracing definition.

Ancient pagan temple, Delphi, Greece.

What then, is Wicca? It is both a spiritual tradition (which is why it is a religion) and a set of practices (which is why it is sometimes called "the Craft"). Some Wiccans honor a god and goddess, while others honor a goddess in whom the two roles are united. We work with the seasons and tides of the Earth, and the rhythms of the Moon, planets and stars. Wiccans see the divine in nature, both within and around us, as we are considered part of nature rather than standing outside of it. In this sense, we see the divine as immanent (meaning "residing within") within nature, and within ourselves. We also have a sense of the spirit of all things that exist, including rocks, trees, animals and places, as well as people. This is why we sometimes refer to them as "beings"—it is because we honor their individual as well as their integral, or "connected," existence. Wiccans place great emphasis on "connection" as we see all matter and all beings as interrelated and interdependent. The symbol for this sense of interconnection is the web—a network of existence through which all beings are linked.

This concept of relatedness is present in all of our rituals and practices, whether spells for healing, rites for marking the seasons, or changes in our lives. If we are part of that wider, connected web, then everything we do affects all things within it. The magical spells we perform key in a particular pattern to be sent further along the

Wicca is a path that emphasizes personal responsibility.

web to effect change. Our rituals are signals that something is happening in our lives, and the full realization of this is felt in our communities and in our everyday experiences. It also affects our everyday actions and colors our approach to ethics and behavior. What we do counts: Shake one part of the web and the whole structure trembles, so we need to be sure that our actions do not harm. An injury to one, to coin a well-known phrase, is an injury to all. A central tenet that unites all Wiccans is attendance to what is known as "the Wiccan Rede," which says: "An it harm none, do thy will" (if it harms none, go ahead). As a moral aspiration, it is a worthy one, and Wicca is a religion that takes a responsible approach to its relationship with all beings.

Wicca is a path that places great responsibility on its followers to acknowledge and appreciate divinity within all nature (including ourselves), to place love and respect at the forefront of our relationship with all beings, and to ensure that harm is caused to none. What it is not is the stereotype that is thankfully dying out; that of the Devil-worshipping monster setting curses to do harm or to gain power over others. Devils are not part of our theology and we go out of our way to avoid harming: Neither make sense in the joyful, celebratory and responsible spiritual path that is Wicca.

Wiccan philosophy and ethics

The word *philosophy* has two distinct meanings: The first describes an approach to life; the second, the formal, academic study of the meaning of life. Wiccan philosophy is certainly concerned with fundamental concepts such as existence, "right" action, knowledge and truth, but tends to be more at home in the looser, more social application of the term—our take on life. Where academic philosophers pursue matters in theory, Wicca takes a more grounded approach. Wiccans are an inquisitive and intelligent bunch, and not averse to deep, philosophical musings, but we

Wiccan ethics incorporate responsibility toward the Earth, our home.

do tend to come back to very basic questions such as how our actions affect our day-to-day lives. In this sense Wiccan philosophy is very much a real world outlook. By way of example, we measure "right" action, not by any inherent morality that the intent allegedly carries, but by its outcome and impact.

There is a very strong impulse within Wicca that looks toward the concept and attainment of balance; not surprising, given the emphasis on our interrelationship with all other beings. Within such a worldview, balance is extremely important. It involves, for example, treading lightly on the Earth, so as not to disturb the environmental web that is currently suffering from the imbalance caused by irresponsible use of its resources.

SEEKING BALANCE

Thinking about balance also encourages a harmonious way of living—pausing to think about the impact we have on other beings raises the question of balance within ourselves and how we might achieve that. This is why Wiccans are interested in self-development; not because we are selfish individualists, but because we know that the need to work on ourselves and our own behavior and understanding is as important as setting the world outside to rights. We are an integral part of that world, and what we do and who we are affects that too. In British traditional Wicca, the four pillars of strength are cited as: "To dare, to will, to know, to keep silence." These four pillars signify the need for witches to develop courage, willpower, willingness to learn and discretion. Balancing ourselves in this way means that we can be brave, act with resolve, keep an open mind, and respect others and the space they inhabit in the world.

The strand within Wicca that exhorts us to pursue self-knowledge alongside our considered and respectful relationship with all beings derives from what our pagan ancestors counted as wisdom. On portals of the temple of Apollo at Delphi are inscribed two exhortations: "Know thyself" and "Nothing in excess." These perhaps best epitomize the approaches that are combined within Wicca; an aspiration for self-knowledge and the attainment of harmony and balance.

Wiccan ethics encourage a sense of inner and outer balance.

21

The Wiccan Rede

"An it harm none, do thy will."

R*ede,* a Middle English word derived from Old English and Old High German, is thought to mean "advice." The Wiccan Rede is a guide to making decisions about how we act. The origins of the Rede are lost in the mists of time and the secrecy to which older working covens were bound, and there is some debate among Wiccan scholars about its historical roots. Its broader meaning, however, is generally agreed; do what you will, but ensure it

The Rede is a guide and foundation to decision-making.

harms no one. What Wiccans may differ on is how far this tenet takes us in considering what "harm" is, who count as the "none" and how far we can practice this simple piece of guidance in a complex world.

Many Wiccans take their spiritual beliefs into the realm of political activism, particularly environmentalism, conservation, animal welfare and social justice. For some of us, if systems, organizations or corporations do harm, then we consider it part of our duty of care toward the Earth and other beings to get them to stop. This extends the interpretation of the Rede to incorporate a duty to prevent or stop harm. To paraphrase Edmund Burke: "The only thing necessary for the triumph of evil is for good people to do nothing." Lack of action, then, can constitute harm.

HARM NONE

What we cannot do, if we are to take the advice of the Wiccan Rede, is cause lesser harms in order to prevent greater harms. If we are to "harm none," then harming none means exactly what it says: The end cannot justify the means if the means are harmful. In short, the means are subject to the same rules as the ultimate goal of an action.

The first part of the Rede, "harm none," is emphasized in Wiccan practice because of its ethical importance. The second part of the Rede is as important. Its first public appearance in 1971 was to a generation rebelling against authority and social conformity, and the advice "do what ye will" was particularly timely. However, the message to follow our own counsel is still relevant; we live in an age where so-called experts line up to tell us what to believe and how to live. The Wiccan Rede reminds us to trust our own good instincts and knowledge above the contemporary tyranny of spin over substance.

Wiccan spirituality

Wicca is a nature religion. It sees the divine in all things, especially in the natural world, and takes the wonderful diversity that is in nature as its guide, celebrating divinity in all its manifestations. For us, nature is sacred because the divine is present within it, and because we are a part of nature, then we too are divine expressions of the God, Goddess or Great Spirit who connects all beings.

The Mother Charge, a recitation by a priestess at esbats, the Full-Moon celebrations at which the Goddess speaks to Her people, declares:

> *I who am the beauty of the green earth,*
> *And the white moon among the stars,*
> *And the mystery of the waters,*
> *Call unto your soul: arise and come unto me,*
> *For I am the soul of nature...*

This encapsulates the importance to witches of the idea of the divine within nature and of nature as the divine. Because of this connection, there is a strong animistic tendency within Wicca, which sees Spirit in all things. Witches are also aware of *genii loci* or "spirits of place," and when we are working magic or doing a circle outdoors, we make sure that we honor the local spirit of the place in which we choose to celebrate.

HONORING THE GODDESS

Wicca is a polytheistic religion—it does not adhere to one god or goddess, but honors the Goddess and God, sometimes Goddess alone in whom the two are united. We also honor various gods and goddesses (deities)—often seen as the Goddess in Her many aspects and names. There is a saying in Wicca that "All

The web is a Wiccan symbol of Spirit and connection.

gods and goddesses are one God or Goddess," to which is sometimes added the acknowledgment "but not all gods and goddesses are the *same* God or Goddess." When we speak of the Goddess or the God we are talking of a being in whom all deities are united. When we speak of Demeter the Earth Goddess, Herne the Horned One, Lugh the Sun God, we see each one as aspects of the God or Goddess and as individual deities in their own right.

Our relationships with our deities are generally close, even intimate. Because we see divinity as being immanent (within), we see our deities as being manifest within us and in the world around us. Since they do not stand apart from humanity or outside of nature and time, our deities are not interventionist—they do not call down judgment or demand sacrifices of us. On the contrary, they are our friends, confidantes, guides, parents, sisters and brothers, upon whom our thinking, feeling and instinctive selves call whenever we feel the need.

Wicca's gods and goddesses are honored as friends and confidantes.

THE GODDESS WITHIN

If you have been used to thinking of the divine as separate from humanity and the everyday world, the idea that you can treat the God or Goddess as a friend might seem quite startling. But if the God or Goddess is a part of us, then we too are the God or Goddess. Talking to the divine in a familiar, friendly manner does not dishonor them; we are simply acknowledging and celebrating the life-affirming relationship we have with them. Of course, the relationship that one develops with the God or Goddess or particular deities is going to be unique and special. Just as we all deal with our personal relationships very differently, there is a variety of attitudes toward the deities within Wicca. But it is true to say that, for the majority of us, there is no contradiction in speaking to the God or Goddess as a friend, and lighting a candle to honor Him or Her.

Wiccan practice varies widely when it comes to the ways in which we conceptualize our deities. There is an approach that sees the God or Goddess as "out there"; present in nature and manifest, for example, as a horned entity, or as a woman clothed in stars. There is another approach that sees the God or Goddess as wholly within nature and within ourselves. A third approach perceives the Deity as representational, as symbolic. For most witches, it is possible to believe all three at once—when I asked a witch friend whether the Deity was within the self, within nature or "out there" as a distinctive entity, she smiled and replied "yes."

LIVING MAGICALLY

Wicca is a religion that combines two important elements: spirituality and magic. Although in most world religions the two are considered separate, in Wicca they are very closely intertwined. At one level, we see all acts of creation as inherently magical. The most amazing magical event was the birth of the Universe. Smaller but no less wondrous examples of such magic take place around us all the time—but because we are so accustomed to them, we do not notice. Rediscovering this magic through learning and experience is part of the spiritual journey; hence the Wiccan interest in country lore, herbs, astronomy, and the rocks, stones and crystals that are the bones of the Earth. We study the ways of trees and the cycle of the seasons and the stars and planets in order to grow in knowledge. Our spirituality is pagan—like our pre-Christian ancestors we revere the spirit and magic of the natural world.

At another level, we acknowledge magic as a conscious act by which we seek both inward and outward transformation. Each magical act changes us in accordance with its nature. Because all things that exist are linked together and because we, too, are the God or Goddess, when we perform healing spells we send out healing to individuals who are also aspects of the whole, as well as effecting change within ourselves. This is linked to our notion of what is spiritual—how we understand our place within and relationship to all beings, the Earth, the Deity, the cosmos. When we call upon the elements, the spirit of nature, the Deity in our magical work, we are also celebrating our spirituality. For witches, magic is a spiritual act.

LOVE IS THE LAW

In Wicca, there is no moralistic doctrine or dogma other than the advice offered in the Wiccan Rede. We are constantly re-evaluating our understanding of what it means to be spirit-in-flesh. We see the body as co-extensive with the spirit, and consequently, as sacred. The Mother Charge tells us "All acts of love and pleasure are my rituals." The only "law" here is love, and acts of love are performed in mutuality, with permission, and not to harm, control or disempower. In Wicca, physical pleasure is an act of worship. As spirit-in-flesh we honor and give value to the body through intense connection with another human being, and in turn connect with the God or Goddess through ecstasy. It matters not whether we are gay, straight, bisexual or transgendered—the physical world is sacred, and in celebrating our physicality, our sexuality and our human nature, we honor the Goddess, giver of all life, and soul of all nature.

The physical world is seen as co-extensive with Spirit, and therefore sacred.

Green witchcraft

It should be obvious by now that Wiccans have a very special bond with nature and the environment. This relationship is one of reverence and responsibility; we cannot venerate the spirit of nature while ignoring the often adverse impact that humans have on our environment. Many of us perceive the Earth-web—the connected strands that link all beings and elements on the planet—as a whole being. Sometimes we call this interconnected biosystem "Gaia," after the primal Earth-mother who gave birth pathenogenically (without insemination) to the Waters, the Sky and the Mountains. Whether we believe in Gaia as a unitary entity or as a symbol of the interdependence of all beings on the planet, we feel responsible for the wellbeing of the Earth.

Hands-on responsibility for the environment is important.

On planet Earth we are all "relations"—people, trees, rivers, animals and birds.

Gaia as a system is in trouble and so are we. The expanding hole in the ozone layer, the rapid changes in our weather systems and rise in global temperatures all signal danger. We know what we need to do: Move toward biodegradability; quit burning fossil fuels and destroying the rain forests; stop pumping wastes into the air, the earth and the water; find safe, sustainable forms of energy. We rely on the survival of the Earth; the health of the planet is important to everyone. As witches, we derive our powers and nourish our spiritual selves through contact with the natural world. Watching our planet home being polluted is very distressing. Seeing our fellow beings—trees, fields and rivers, animals and birds—facing destruction is extremely difficult. All of these beings are our "relations;" for witches, they are neighbors and friends with whom we seek to co-exist.

THE FIVE ELEMENTS

As well as seeing our God or Goddess and ourselves as part of nature, in Wicca we use a system of five elements from which all existence is derived. These elements are Air, Fire, Water, Earth and Spirit. The physical manifestation of Air in the natural world is the atmosphere of the planet, the air we breathe and the ozone layer that filters out the potentially harmful rays of the Sun. Fire is seen in the warmth of the Sun and the temperature needed to keep all things in balance. Water is in the rains that nourish the crops and vegetation, in the streams, rivers, seas and oceans. The Earth is found in the rocks, mountains, valleys and underground caverns. The fifth element, Spirit, is that which connects all these together to form the balanced system that is Gaia. However, when the balance of the elements is out of kilter, the delicate web of life is endangered, and in order to save our spiritual and physical home from harm, we are obliged to act.

PRACTICAL ACTION

Because we are practical people, this action means we must do more than stand in circles casting healing spells for the planet. Consequently, most witches have a very involved approach toward saving the Earth. This may take the form of practical, collective activity, such as neighborhood litter collection, beach clearances, reclaiming and planting abandoned patches or lots in the locality, or broader, more overtly political activity such as protests, petitions or other contributions to environmental campaigns. This is in addition to organizing our own households so that we conserve water, recycle paper, cans and glass, and shop responsibly for environmentally friendly products.

Taking responsibility for the Earth means practical involvement.

One very positive activity that many witches get involved with is tree planting. Not only does this provide good exercise and get us outdoors, it can often be instructive, especially when meeting people with a great deal of knowledge and experience of the natural environment. It is not unusual, on a tree-planting mission, to combine planting with a ritual or blessing for the trees we are bedding-in. This encourages us to remember the bond we share with all our relations and helps us to link with the Earth and its growth cycles.

Witches see the natural world as a magical place. When we drum on sea-shores, chant in the woods or dance around standing stones that our ancestors used to mark the passage of the stars and planets, we find ways to harmonize with the spirits of nature. However, we are all deeply aware that drumming, chanting and dancing alone are not enough, and that in order to save the environment, we have to take responsibility and act accordingly.

It is important to make connections with your natural surroundings.

Life, death and rebirth

Because Wicca is a nature religion, witches have an approach to the cycles of life and death that reflect our understanding of natural processes. We perceive that in nature all things are born, change and die from their given forms to become something new. A flower grows, blooms, dies and returns to Earth as compost. A rock is born out of the magma that flows in the centre of the Earth as it cools, then time, wave and weather wear it down and eventually it is crushed

The transition from life to death and rebirth is marked on the ancient landscape.

to dust or sand. As the Universe expands, a pocket of gas becomes dense and gives birth to a star of stunning luminosity, which eventually burns itself out, collapses inwards and explodes in a supernova, without which there would be no carbon, oxygen or other essential life-giving elements in the Universe. We humans are born, change, die and transform, and in Wicca we speak of this final stage as rebirth.

REINCARNATION

Some witches take this literally to mean reincarnation—back in the body—and certainly some Wiccan practices echo this belief. For example, the *Legend of the Goddess*, a story-led ritual used in some Alexandrian covens, mentions that to be reborn "...you must die and be made ready for a new body..." Some witches claim to recognize some of their fellow coveners from previous lives and use this as a way to explain their spiritual and magical affinity. Reincarnation is a belief more associated with ancient Middle and Far Eastern religions than those of the West, and links more closely to a worldview that perceives spirit and body as separate. Initially, reincarnation beliefs may seem contradictory in a religion that unites and celebrates spirit-in-body. However, Wicca's take on reincarnation has a background of Celtic mythology and ancestor practice attached, which helps to make sense of coming "back to the body."

LAND OF THE EVER-YOUNG

Some witches speak of those who have died as having "passed over to the Summerlands." In Celtic mythology, this is the land of the ever-young, where healing waters flow and the old, the sick and those who have suffered are restored. In the Arthurian legends, King Arthur is escorted to the Isles of the Blessed in a barge, tended by nine maidens, representing the triple Goddess of the land. Although Celtic mythology does not make explicit mention of coming back from the Summerlands, it is possible to see how those who believe in

Ancient burial site in Scandinavia.

reincarnation interpret this as a place of "being made ready for a new body," a form of spiritual recycling, perhaps. In addition, there is evidence from ancient burial sites that are notably womblike in shape that the burial rituals of our pagan ancestors may have accommodated the notion of reincarnation. Placing the dead back into the Earth may have seemed like the planting of seeds which came back to growth in the next season from the Earth Mother.

SPIRAL OF TRANSFORMATION

However, many witches do not believe in reincarnation at all, but interpret rebirth as part of the process of constant change that characterizes all things in the Universe. In this view, life, death and rebirth are points on a spiral, rather than fixed points in a circle that characterize most reincarnation beliefs. Instead of seeing the movement of existence as a single line that passes in a circle to return to the same spot, the "spiral" view takes us through cycles to a different place and a different form of being. Although all things in the Universe are born into a given form, change and then decay or degrade, nothing is really completely destroyed. What takes place is transformation—the process of moving from one state or form into another.

Following this line of thought, we can see that the star that is born, collapses and explodes is not wiped off the face of the Universe but takes a new form in oxygen and carbon, which in turn make other life possible. Witches who believe in rebirth rather than reincarnation believe that when the knowing, conscious span of our lives is spent, we die and decompose into a new form which continues as part of the whole. This happens with flowers, rocks, stars and everything else in nature, so it would be odd if humans were exempt from this process. Some witches believe that just as the physical returns to nourish the Earth, so our individual conscious selves dissolve into the collective soul of the Universe—the Goddess. We do not cease to be, but become another life form, entering another state of being.

In this worldview, the mapping of the planets that our ancestors left behind in their monuments and standing stones, the spiral, maze and labyrinth patterns carved into prehistoric burial sites, make perfect sense. In a world that saw the cyclical rise and fall of the cereal harvest, from seed through stalk and fruit to seed again, burial of the ancestors in an Earth womb was natural. Archaeologists suspect that the bones of some ancestors were removed at particular times, possibly to witness the ceremonies of the living or to represent the spiritual presence of the ancestors. This occasional removal of bones from the Earth-womb does not tally with the idea that they were being planted symbolically in order to regenerate and come to be reborn again. Rather, it speaks of a different understanding about what was miraculous about life and the impulse of regeneration—the ancestors as our progenitors and the living as future ancestors.

MAPPING THE MYSTERY OF LIFE AND DEATH

Taking this view, the meaning of the mystical spirals that turn up on tombs and ceremonial stones in the form of mazes and labyrinths is found within us rather than in our expected resurrection. The mysteries of birth, death and rebirth are found not in the expectation that the dead will return, but in the fact that we are the dead, returned.

WHAT IS WICCA?

The spark of creation, of genesis that created those presently living comes from our predecessors. There was a time when we, as individual conscious beings, did not exist; this is very difficult for us to fully understand, because we have to imagine it from a point in our own existence. This is the mystery of the spiral— the spark that exists within the babe in the womb, who will one day carry a babe in her womb or produce a child of his body. The spiral does not, by definition, join up in completion, but runs into a centre and out again—the state of constant flux that perfectly describes the movement of the Universe. The spirals, mazes and labyrinthine patterns that our ancestors chose to place on sites where the dead were housed represented a mystery of life—and this fundamental realization foreshadowed both the discovery of the double-helix spiral of DNA and the spiralling shapes of galaxies. The mysteries of life and death lie within us, as well as around us.

Standing stone circle, Callanish, Scotland.

The Wiccan cosmos

Because Wicca is a mystery religion, as well as a nature religion, our relationship with the Universe is one of constantly unfolding revelation. We call it a mystery religion because we know that some things can only be understood through the direct experience of the individual. What we learn through such experiences is sometimes very hard for individuals to articulate, and others to comprehend. A description of a Wiccan view of the cosmos, therefore, is bound to present itself as far more mundane than the experience, and what follows should be understood as an invitation to find out for yourself rather than a definitive map.

As a child I would write after my name and address in exercise books: "England, Europe, the World, the Galaxy, the Universe." I often think that it takes adults a long time to relearn the wisdom that was natural to us as children, and this is just such an instance. The desire to know our place in the Universe is an important element of spiritual journeying. Knowing where we are also brings us closer to who we are, what our purpose is and why that matters.

In the Wiccan cosmos, our pagan spirituality tells us that we are of nature; this is a vital clue to finding our cosmic "address." We are human animals who, in common with other animals, depend upon the natural resources of the planet for our survival. But what does it mean to be an animal that has a capacity for abstract thought and language, is aware of its individual consciousness and its own search for spiritual meaning?

Such questions are the first step along the way to spiritual discovery, but they can only be answered through the experience of the journey itself. In Wicca, it is this journey itself that is the meaning. This is implied by the child's natural

The spiritual journey begins with questions about our place in the cosmos.

New witches are encouraged to learn more about the solar year.

tendency to start at the beginning and work outward in steps until we reach the Universe. Seeing nature as a continuum, rather than something that stops outside our front doors, is something that we have to relearn.

RHYTHMS OF THE WORLD

In Wicca, newcomers are encouraged to learn a little basic physics regarding the place of the Earth in the solar system and the physical interaction of the Sun and the Moon with the Earth's seasons and tides in order to better understand the natural rhythms with which we work.

MARKERS OF THE SACRED CYCLE

The Earth's tilt is the basis of the seasons—the inclination of its axis means that at times we are closer to the Sun and as the temperature and the weather change on a cyclical basis, so the vegetation and life on the planet respond. In the Wiccan year, there are four solar festivals. These are markers of astronomical events; the shortest and longest days at the winter and summer solstices and the two days of perfect balance between the hours of daylight and darkness at the spring and autumn equinoxes. In the northern hemisphere the shortest day at the winter solstice usually falls on December 21 or 22, the longest day at the summer solstice on June 21 or 22, the spring equinox on March 21 or 22 and the autumn equinox on September 21 or 22. In the southern hemisphere the solstices and the equinoxes are reversed. These events are seen as four struts on the wheel of the year, important markers of the sacred cycle.

THE LUNAR CYCLE

The Moon, our closest celestial neighbor, produces the tides on the waters of Earth and influences the reproductive cycles of some animals. The full cycle of the Moon through its phases from new (or dark) Moon, first quarter, half, full, last quarter and back to new or dark again is 29.5 days. Although the word *month* is taken from the word *moon*, our calendar does not faithfully follow lunar cycles, of which there are thirteen rather than twelve in a year.

One of the first things that people learn about the Craft is the importance to witches of the lunar cycles for the timing of spells and rituals. Similarly, some activities and spells are timed with the seasons, set in relation to the Earth's dance around the Sun.

The wonder of the cyclical relationships of Earth, Sun, Moon and stars inspires and moves us closer to knowledge of ourselves and our place in the cosmos. In Wicca we try to carry out our research on the physical, experience it for ourselves and express it poetically.

The lunar cycle is particularly important to witches.

Life cycles

The sense of change in the biological and social events of our own lives is also celebrated in Wicca. Accordingly, witches celebrate a number of aspects of the human life cycle as sacred and special.

In common with others, witches celebrate the three common rites of passage—birth, marriage and death—with naming ceremonies, marriage or "handfasting" ceremonies and funeral rites. These are the most commonly recognized life-cycle events in Western societies. Other aspects of our biological and social life cycles that are not as commonly celebrated, however, are highly valued in Wicca.

Witches celebrate many aspects of change in our life cycles.

A birth is regarded as a blessing, and childhood, a time when we interact with the world in simple, immediate terms, is seen as particularly sacred. But we also value the transition from childhood to puberty, adolescence and adulthood, as part of the constant change that marks our lives. In most Western societies, the biological changes from girlhood to womanhood, from boyhood to manhood, are not marked or celebrated. Indeed, the whole issue of menstruation, let alone the menarche (first menstrual period) is generally a secretive process, where silence rather than celebration rules. In Wicca, we celebrate a young woman's first moon-blood, because we see this as a sacred event. Sometimes we celebrate the deepening of a young man's voice, so that he can join the world of men in a positive way, rather than in the negative ways that "manliness" is conferred in patriarchal societies.

Our handfasting ceremonies commonly include vows that hold for either a year and a day or for as long as love lasts. This is in recognition that people continue changing after they fall in love, and that a vow to stay together for eternity may not reflect this. We also honor aging with "croning" ceremonies for post-menstrual women and "elderhood" ceremonies for older men as we see wisdom as the gift of age, and value this aspect of our lives. In our spirituality, death is seen as part of a process of transformation rather than the end of our existence, and so we honor, remember and speak with our loved ones on the Day of the Dead every year.

In Wicca we ask the blessing of the Goddess on newborns, invoke Her to accompany the dead to their rest and ask Her to midwife us to rebirth. Throughout our changes, the only thing constant is Her love.

The beauty of ageing is respected and honored.

The sacred landscape

O ur spirituality in Wicca brings us in touch with the divine within nature, and consequently our sacred places can be found in the natural world and in the landscape. These are sometimes at sites created by our ancient pagan ancestors that marked the passage of the stars and planets, the cycles of Earth, Moon and Sun and even the rites of our own life cycles.

Although all nature is sacred, witches hold some places in special regard. Our spirituality is inspired by that of our pre-Christian ancestors, who left clues to what they praised, honored or found important dotted all around the landscape. Around the world, there are hundreds of sites where our ancestors raised stone cairns or earthworks, carved animal shapes into hillsides, placed stones in circles, pyramids, avenues and trilithons, painted ritual scenes on cave walls, carved holy symbols into rocks, maintained ash or oak-groves or tended and decorated wells. They must have sensed that some places in the landscape were special, seeing them as gateways to a magical otherworld in which priests, witches, shamans and cunning-folk could use to walk between the worlds.

Alternatively, these may have been places particularly associated with the gifts and blessings of particular deities.

Today, many of us still feel the ancient and very human urge to visit these sacred sites and pay our respects to the ancestors and to the deities. We sit in the stone circles, or touch and commune with the ancient sites in order to get closer to the impulse that drove our ancestors to create them. Some of us like to leave small devotional offerings, such as flowers, coins, grain or incense, to honor the

locus genii or spirit of place. Often we leave these gifts to let the spirits or deities of that place know that they are still remembered and honored.

There are also natural places in the world, shaped without human design, that are still considered as focal points for the divine presence. These are the mountainsides, hilltops, waterfalls and springs where people are drawn at different times of the year to make offerings or celebrate together. The impulse to mark some sites as sacred may be an ancient one, but it is also present and continuous.

Avebury Stone Circle,
Wiltshire, England.

THE EIGHT SABBATS

The year's wheel

Our ancestors acknowledged the human relationship with the Earth's seasonal round by marking particular points in the year's turning with celebrations. The remnants of many folk customs indicate the importance placed upon human interconnectedness with nature, the flow and ebb of the tides and seasons of Earth's solar revolution. In Wicca, the strands of these customs have been reclaimed and woven into the eight festivals of the Wiccan year, known as the Sabbats.

The eight sabbats

Festival	Northern hemisphere	Southern hemisphere
Samhain	October 31	May 1
Yule (winter solstice)	December 21/22	June 21/22
Imbolc	February 1/2	August 1/2
Ostara (spring equinox)	March 21/22	September 21/22
Beltane	May 1	October 31
Litha (summer solstice)	June 21/22	December 21/22
Lughnasadh	August 1/2	February 1/2
Modron (autumn equinox)	September 21/22	March 21/22

Of the eight festivals that witches celebrate, four are based directly on the astronomical events produced by Gaia's 23.45° tilt: the winter and summer solstices and the spring and autumn equinoxes. The dates of the eight Sabbat festivals of the northern hemisphere are reversed in the southern hemisphere (see box opposite) to take account of the fact that the southern hemisphere experiences winter while the north experiences summer, and so on.

THE SOLAR FESTIVALS

The four solar festivals have special names in Wiccan tradition. The winter solstice is known as Yule and comes from a Scandinavian word *Yul* meaning "wheel." We assume that our Nordic ancestors perceived this as a time of stillness and completion, a point on the turning wheel of the year that completed a cycle. The summer solstice is known as *Litha* and the origin of this

Some festivals are marked by nature's changes rather than by the calendar.

word is more obscure. Strangely, it is also thought to mean "wheel," though perhaps for different reasons (see pages 68–69). The spring or vernal equinox, sometimes called the "Festival of Trees," is best known in Wicca as Ostara. The festival is named for a Teutonic goddess of fertility (in Anglo-Saxon *Eostre*), and celebrates the return of growth and new birth to the Earth. The autumn equinox is known as *Modron*, meaning "mother." Modron is the All-Mother, the fertile, fecund and nurturing aspect of the Goddess, appropriate to the season of fruitfulness.

If we imagine the year as a wheel, with Yule in the north and Litha in the south (reverse in the southern hemisphere), the other two solar festivals are planted squarely on the perpendicular. Crosswise to these, and intersecting each of the solar festivals, are the four Sabbats known as the Celtic fire festivals. Although roughly attached to calendar dates, these are slightly more movable feasts and some witches prefer to mark these when particular plants appear or the first appropriate lunation thereafter, usually the first Full Moon.

CELTIC FIRE FESTIVALS

The first of these, moving around the wheel east to west from the winter solstice, is Imbolc (pronounced im-molk), meaning "ewe's milk." Traditionally, this is the festival celebrated when the first snowdrops appear or the first Full Moon thereafter (see dates for both hemispheres in the box on page 50). It has strong associations with the Celtic fire goddess Brighid (pronounced breed), sometimes called Brigit or Bride/Bridie, and is often called the Feast of

The winter solstice marks both stillness and change.

*The pagan
festivals mark the
rhythms of nature.*

THE EIGHT SABBATS

Brighid. Imbolc marks the quickening of the Earth, the first thaws after winter, the birth of the lambs and the first signs that spring is coming. Continuing around the wheel, between Ostara and Litha, is Beltane (pronounced either bell-tayne or bile-tin), meaning "bright fire." Beltane is celebrated when the first May-blossom blooms or on the first Full Moon thereafter (see dates for both hemispheres in the box on page 50). Beltane celebrates the greening of the Earth and all aspects of fertility in vegetation, birds and animals, and is associated with the Green Man, a spirit or god of nature.

Between Litha and Modron comes *Lughnasadh* (pronounced loo-na-sah) or Lammas, celebrated when the first corn sheaf is cut or the first Full Moon after that (see dates for both hemispheres in the box on page 50). Lughnasadh celebrates the cereal harvest and the gathering in of blessings and honors the spirit of plenty that brings the corn to ripeness. Finally, between Modron and Yule is the Sabbat known as *Samhain* (pronounced sow-ain) meaning "first frost." As its name suggests, this is sometimes celebrated when the first frosts come, or on the first Full Moon thereafter (see dates for both hemispheres in the box on page 50). This is the Feast of the Ancestors, the Day of the Dead and also the old Celtic New Year, where we leave the warmer days behind and go down into the darkness that will lead us back to Yule.

It is an old tradition, for the Celtic fire festivals at least, that the festival begins at sundown the day before and ends on the following sundown. This means that if you celebrate Beltane on May 1, the festival actually begins at sundown on April 30.

These, then, are the eight great Wiccan Sabbats, the radials of the year's wheel. Exploring the customs and the meanings of the various festivals will help you to understand more about pagan spirituality. Experiencing for yourself the way that witches work with Gaia's many tides and seasons will also help you to attune to the spirit of nature and understand better the changes and shifts that occur in your own life.

THE EIGHT SABBATS

You will find, as you explore the festivals in more depth, that each Sabbat is a still moment that we create on a wheel that represents a constant state of flux. Litha celebrates the longest day of the year, but carries within it the message that the hours of daylight will afterward diminish. The spring equinox brings a perfect balance of light with darkness, but thereafter we tip over into the season of greatest light. The same is true of all the solar festivals, and at a more subtle level, the Celtic fire festivals. Each marks events in the Earth's seasonal cycle and each carries the seeds of its own demise. You will learn for yourself the deeper spiritual lessons that the Sabbats impart as you follow the cycle around.

The cycle of life, death and renewal can be seen all around us.

Samhain—
the Festival of the Dead

Celebrated on the last day of October in the northern hemisphere and the first day of May in the southern, Samhain stands halfway between the autumn equinox Modron and Yule. It is sometimes seen as the beginning of winter, but it is also the Festival of the Dead, when we remember and honor the ancestors. It is a magical time when the veil between the worlds of the dead and the living is thin, and in Wicca we celebrate death as a part of life, and to give positive value to the idea of going into the dark.

Our Celtic ancestors saw Samhain as a key point of the year's turning, a chance to begin anew. The eighth-century scholarly monk Bede noted that custom named November the "blood month," and he attributed this to the slaughter of beasts in preparation for winter provisions. With the surplus from summer burned on a balefire, our peace made with the dead and preparations made for the winter, our ancestors may well have seen this as a key departure point from the old cycle into the new. This is why pagans today refer to this festival as the Celtic New Year. Although Samhain is literally "first frost," and thus the first of the winter festivals, it also marks preparation for change.

Pumpkins are often used to create lantern "faces" for the Samhain festivities.

This is the season of the Hag Goddess, associated with nocturnal creatures.

CELEBRATING THE CRONE GODDESS

The season is associated with ghosts, spirits and the dead walking. It is the season of the Hag or *Calliach* (Scots Gaelic meaning "old woman"), the crone aspect of the Goddess who midwives us, with great compassion, from life to death. She is Rhiannon, goddess of transition, Ceridwen, goddess of the cauldron of transformation, and Hecate, weaver of wisdom and guardian at the crossroads. The Crone Goddess is celebrated to some extent in the plastic masks and costumes that children wear at Halloween.

Nowadays, witches celebrate by holding a ritual in which we name, honor, remember and speak with the dead. Beginning with those who have died in the last year, we move on to family and friends and then commemorate all our ancestors. Then, out of grief, we bring back joy and name the newborn babies of the last year, the new friends and opportunities we have met. Samhain serves as a reminder that life contains death, but it also contains the mystery of rebirth and the movement of the cycle ever onward.

Yule—the winter solstice

Sometimes called midwinter, Yule marks the shortest day and, since the worst days of winter are usually to follow, is more accurately mid-year. The sixteenth-century poet John Donne called this time "the year's midnight," when "the world's whole sap is sunk." However, Yule carries within it a paradox—just as the winter solstice commemorates the annual demise of the Sun's powers, it witnesses its rebirth. This is why Yule is also known as "Sun-return."

Yule is the time when the Goddess labors to bring forth the Star Child, and Yule was called "Mothernight" by our northern European ancestors. For witches who celebrate God and Goddess, this is the Solar God who, by the time of Ostara, will

The winter solstice is a time of repose and rebirth.

grow into the young man who impregnates the young, fertile aspect of the Goddess, and another Star Child who will succeed him the following Yule.

The holly is the sacred plant of protection.

SOLAR REBIRTH

However we see it, the symbolism of this solar rebirth is mirrored in our celebrations. At the darkest time, when the Earth seems bare and forlorn, we bring evergreens into our homes—holly for protection, ivy for the faithful promise that life endures, mistletoe for fertility. In the first days of winter, these remind us that Earth will be green again. We feast to lighten our hearts and share the fellowship of others to warm ourselves from within when all around seems bleak. The importance to us of human company at Yule is evident in the numbers who travel to sacred sites to witness sunrise or sunset together. Members of my own group organize a community ceilidh—a social gathering with folk music and dance—to celebrate Yule and bring some of its message to our local community.

Although the surface of the Earth is denuded of its most luxurious greenery in the dark season, below the surface seeds are sleeping, ready for germination. Witches take their cue from this to use the darkest time to delve into the deeper places of our minds and spirits, to meditate and bring back new ideas, projects and developments in our lives. In our rituals to mark Yule, we look for the invisible Sun; the vital inner spark which, reenergized, will keep our spirits and our physical energy going through the winter. The candles we light to rekindle the fires of Sol also symbolize our desire to relight our inner Sun. "As above; so below," as the Wise say.

Imbolc—the feast of Brighid

By Imbolc the days are noticeably longer and signs that winter is loosening its grip can be seen. The first shoots are pushing through the soil and snowdrops, the "Maids of February," are gracing gardens and woodlands. Imbolc marks the birth of the first lambs and the ewes begin to lactate; hence the association of the festival with milking. In one old song, "Ailse Ban," a milkmaid soothes the cow she is milking by assuring her that "the Holy St. Bridget" herself is milking "the white *kye* (clouds) in heaven."

Imbolc marks the emergence of the first snowdrops.

The "St. Bridget" in question is a Christianized version of the Irish fire goddess Brighid, whose immense popularity could not be eradicated by Christianity. Even among pagans today, Brighid is a much-beloved goddess, and Imbolc seen as her festival. Brighid's role as fierce protector of women, children and newborn animals is reflected in Christian mythology, where St. Bridget is the reputed midwife to Mary. In Wicca, she is midwife to the spring, the divine woman who breathes her fiery breath upon the Earth to awaken it. Her role extends to enabling new projects—many of us plant seeds and bulbs at this time to represent areas in our lives that we wish to nurture and grow.

SECRET RITES

Imbolc is very much a women's festival, and, traditionally, for the first part of the celebration, women practice their own rites which are never spoken of outside the circle or when men are present. The men, of course, have their own mysteries to practice while they wait to be invited into the circle as honored guests. They bring gifts for Brighid, which are laid at the feet of a *bridiog*—an effigy of the goddess that is dressed and decorated by the women and placed in a basket. Throughout the ritual, celebrants may approach the *bridiog* to whisper to her their secrets and wishes.

Brighid is a goddess of healing, inspiration of poets and patron of blacksmiths and metalworkers. She is the fire in the head of poets and the fire in the belly of those who act upon their ideas—a goddess of inspiration and action. As patron of metalworkers, she is the key to turning raw materials into useful and beautiful things—a goddess of transformation. At Imbolc, a time of renewal, we celebrate changes around and within us, and renew our commitment to making the world a better place. We honor the spark of divine creativity within us and raise healing energy.

The Chalice Well at Chalice Well Garden in Glastonbury, England.

Ostara—the vernal equinox

Ostara marks the vernal (meaning youthful) equinox—a time of balance between daylight and darkness, the point before day is longer than night. It falls in the Christian season of Lent in the northern hemisphere (see the box on page 50 for dates in the southern hemisphere), which itself comes from an Anglo-Saxon word, referring to the lengthening of the days.

It is also a celebration of growth and derives its name from a German goddess whose totem was the hare. The saying "Mad as a March hare" comes from observations of their mating behavior at this time of year, as they appear to "box" and leap about in the fields. In fact, hares are no more crazy in their behavior in March than at any other time; it is just that the grass is short enough for their antics to be visible! The hare is seen as prolifically fertile and many Moon goddesses linked with women's reproductive cycles share it as a totem of

The hare is sacred to the goddess of the Moon.

earthy sexuality and fecundity. Today's Easter Bunny is a bowdlerized descendant of this early pagan fertility symbol, but is nonetheless regarded with fondness by witches who recognize it as a modern remnant of an ancient tradition.

SYMBOL OF FERTILITY AND RENEWAL

Eggs have been linked with this time of year for thousands of years. This enduring, pre-Christian symbol of fertility, renewal and the life-force inspires pagans today to celebrate by decorating eggs for the Ostara celebrations. Sometimes these hollow, painted eggs are hung on a branch placed in the centre of our sacred spaces. This is a branch thrown by the winter or early spring winds and should never be cut from a living tree. As the eggs represent life-in-potential, we magically imbue them with wishes we hope will manifest during the coming summer.

Ostara is a good time to be out in nature and witness for ourselves the effects of the sap rising in the trees, the buds and the busy behavior of nesting birds. It is a time to visit the daffodils—the flower of this festival—in their natural setting, and discover why they are called harbingers of spring. It is also an ideal time to seek balance in our own lives; in our celebrations, we sometimes walk between a black candle and a white one, and pause before we pass through this gateway into summer, to ask the God or Goddess what we can do to restore the balance in our lives that will enable us to grow.

Eggs represent fertility and potential.

Beltane—the time of the Green Man

The feast of Beltane celebrates the coming of summer. It is the time when we honor the Green Man, consort of the Goddess and ancient spirit of the Greenwood. Known as "Jack-in-the-Green" or "Robin," he joins with Marian, his May Queen.

Maypoles are ancient symbols of fertility.

> *Hal an tow, jolly rumble oh*
> *We were up long before the day oh*
> *To welcome in the summer*
> *To welcome in the may oh*
> *The summer is a-comin' in*
> *And winter's gone away oh'*

"HAL-AN-TOW." TRAD. ENGLISH MAYING SONG

This is the season of Herne, protector of the Greenwood and symbol of fertility, growth and change. Just as buck deer shed their antlers following mating in May, with the Goddess pregnant with the Star Child, Herne declares his readiness to forsake his wanderings and take his place beside her. On Beltane Eve, some witches take to the woods, to "bring in" the May-blossom at dawn. For our ancestors, this was a time of sexual licence, so possibly "bringing in the May" was a euphemism for a more traditional activity of Beltane. Unsurprisingly, many pagan handfastings and marriages take place at this festival.

CLOSE TO THE FAIRY WORLD

In the wheel of the year, Beltane stands opposite Samhain; just as at Samhain when the veil between the worlds of the living and the dead is thin, at Beltane the world of mortals and that of faery are very close. The fairy Otherworld was well-known by our ancestors, who left us stories of seers and poets who gained their gifts after falling asleep under a hawthorn, May-tree or fairy-mound.

Our Celtic ancestors drove cattle between two sacred fires on May 1 to protect them before sending them out to pasture; this was the *bel-tine*, the "lucky" or "bright" fire. The feast may also be named for a northern European god or goddess named Bel/Belenos/Belissama. The Celtic preface *bel* means "bright," indicating that this god or goddess had solar connections.

Whatever the festival's origins, the sacred fire features strongly in Wiccan celebrations. If celebrating outdoors, we light a small bonfire which the sprightly can leap to obtain a Beltane blessing. Sometimes a broomstick is used instead, symbolizing the sacred conjunction of male (handle) and female (brush), and marking the threshold between spring and summer. As we cross it, we make promises to keep in the coming year.

Fires are set at Beltane to bring luck and blessings.

Litha—the summer solstice

Although the best of summer is usually yet to come, the summer solstice marks the height of the Sun's powers on the longest day of the year. This is the time to gather strength from the Sun before the hours of daylight begin to diminish over the next six months. Like Yule, the festival of Litha carries within it a paradox; the moment we celebrate the Sun's powers at their greatest is the very moment those powers begin to wane. This reminds us of an essential physical and spiritual truth—that our festivals are fleeting instants of stillness on the wheel of change and are themselves symbols of the constant flux that is the nature of all existence.

The word *Litha* is supposed to mean "wheel," though its origins are obscure. There may be a link, however, with a custom first recorded two thousand years ago, of setting a wheel alight and rolling it downhill, representing, presumably, the fall of the Sun at the height of its powers. There might also have been an element of sympathetic magic here; symbolically sending the Sun down to warm the fields and thus urge the growth of the crops in the coming season. Certainly there is a strong association with fire at midsummer—which, like Yule, is more accurately termed "mid-year" with the best of the weather yet to come. Bonfires have been lit and torches carried around hillsides at this time for at least the last seven centuries, and one suspects for much earlier, before written records of these practices were made.

Litha is usually celebrated outdoors, weather permitting, and usually witches gather at the old sacred sites—the standing stones, circles and hillsides—in order to observe the solstice sunrise with others. Many of us set off on the evening of

June 20 (December 20 in the southern hemisphere) to keep vigil together until sunrise on the next day. This means staying awake during the shortest night, and keeping each other entertained with stories and songs after drumming the sun down below the horizon at sunset. At dawn, we begin drumming again, this time to encourage old Sol's exertions to rise early, ride high and shine long and bright upon the longest day. The rest of the day is usually spent outside, sharing rituals and food, catching up on lost sleeping—and getting home.

The Hele Stone at Stonehenge in Wiltshire, England marks the point of sunrise on the summer solstice.

Lughnasadh —
the harvest festival

Lughnasadh falls between the summer solstice, when the Sun's strength is greatest, and the autumn equinox, when daylight and darkness are of equal length. It celebrates the cereal harvest and its alternative name, Lammas, is thought to come from the Anglo-Saxon *Hlaef-mass* meaning "loaf mass." The title "Lughnasadh," however, derives from the name of the Irish God Lugh whom contemporary pagans honor as a Sun deity, and this harvest festival marks the gathering in of the grains ripened by his or her rays.

Corn dollies represent the spirit of the corn.

For our ancient ancestors, the cycle of cereal crops represented something altogether more mysterious; the growth, fall and rebirth of the grain reflected the human cycle of birth, death and continuation. Carvings representing corn can be found in ancient burial sites, indicating its spiritual as well as its material significance. The spirit of the corn had to be propitiated and tempted back to the fields, and it is known from documented customs of more recent centuries that a couple would make love in a field shorn of corn in order to enact the regeneration of the crops. The mysterious but potent corn spirit was lured into and captured by the woven corn dollies that feature at this festival, also known as "spirit cages."

This is the time of John Barleycorn, the caring father aspect of the god who was wedded to the pregnant Goddess in May, and is now cut down as the harvest, to feed the people. Some witches see the harvest as a gift from the Mother Goddess, who shares her body to nourish her children. Again we see one of the contradictions innate within the festivals; the time of plenty and celebration is also the time of cutting down and sacrifice. Lammas fairs still exist in parts of England, remnants of a time when the cereal harvest was greeted with great jubilation.

It is hard for city-dwellers, who have the privilege of the year-round availability of nutritious food, to understand the importance of the harvest to people for whom the staple stock from last year may have run out many weeks before. At Lammas, the time of gathering in the blessings we reap from the

planting, we are reminded also of the importance of its distribution. Consequently, some witches combine their enjoyment of feasting and celebrating this time of plenty with a commitment to giving back either through money or charitable or political work, to ensure a fair harvest for all.

The blessings of the harvest are celebrated at Lughnasadh.

modron—
the autumnal equinox

At the west of the year's compass stands Modron, like Ostara a day when daylight and darkness are of equal length. Unlike Ostara, however, which brings the promise of longer days, the autumn equinox foreshadows the darker days to come. Modron is the harvest of the fruits of the Earth Mother, who in her aspect as eternal Goddess enters the third trimester of her pregnancy.

For witches who honor God and Goddess, this is the time when the dying Sun God begins his journey across the western ocean to sojourn with the eldest aspect of the Goddess, in the land of the dead at Samhain. Witches can see within the Arthurian legends echoes of the dying god in the fallen King Arthur, who is borne westwards toward either the Summerlands or Avalon, the Celtic Otherworld, accompanied by three, sometimes nine maidens, thought to symbolize the triple Goddess. His renewal is seen in the birth of the Star Child at the winter solstice and his rapid growth to youth, hero and protector in the next year's cycle.

Apple trees are thought to mark boundaries between the worlds.

THE MYSTERY WITHIN

The connection between Avalon—the "Isle of Apples"—and Modron continues with some of the celebrations of Modron today. In our rituals, we slice open apples to reveal

Modron is the year's sunset.

the mystery within—a five-pointed star symbolizing all elements of life combined. We eat them to remind us that, as witches, we walk between worlds; that of consensual reality and that of the magical Otherworld. At this festival, we stand between the pillars of light and darkness, ready to descend, with all those goddesses whose myths are associated with the Underworld, into the long night of the year. We eat the fruits of liminality, and like Inanna, Persephone, Freya and Ishtar, prepare ourselves for the descent into the deep, creative darkness of the six months to follow. Just as seeds germinate in the darkness of the rich earth, we continue to grow by preparing ourselves for stillness in the dark, reaching into the deep places of regeneration within, and bringing back the treasures of creativity and spiritual knowledge.

If Yule is the year's midnight, Modron is its sunset and in this dusk we carry what we can of the Sun's noonday strength at Litha with us into the dark. After Modron we continue toward Samhain, and having travelled the sacred wheel of the year, continue the cycle around.

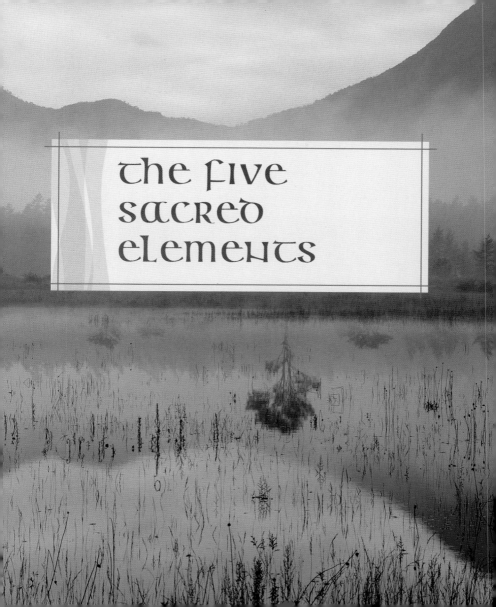

the five sacred elements

The elements

In Classical Greece, where philosophy, physics, and religion were indivisible, our ancestors believed that all material existence in the Universe was divided into five separate elements. These were the elements of Air, Fire, Water and Earth. The fifth was variously postulated as "Love," "Ether" or "Quintessence." Various cultures have at different times marked similar distinctions between the elements of life. The European Celts, for example, honored three sacred

The five sacred elements—Air, Fire, Water, Earth and Spirit—are the basis of all existence.

elements, Earth, Fire and Water, represented by the triskeles, the three-armed symbols found carved at ancient sites, while some classifications in ancient south Asian traditions included Air, Fire, Water and Earth.

Witches today honor the five sacred elements of which the Universe is composed: Air, Fire, Water, Earth and Spirit. Although these can be seen in their raw form—Air as the gas we breathe, Fire as flame, Water as H_2O, Earth as rock—these first four elements are also experienced as components of complex forms. A tree, for example, is composed of Earth (soil, plant matter), Water (sap and tapped moisture), Fire (photosynthesis and the heat that initiates growth and regeneration), and Air (it creates oxygen from carbon dioxide).

The fifth element, Spirit—that which connects all things—causes the first four elements to conjoin in particular proportions and forms to produce life and the Universe as we experience it. Spirit is the sacred weaver of the elements and as "the connection" is, along with the other four, an equal cause and part of the Universe. It is also the great web of life that joins all beings to each other.

ACCESSING THE DIVINE WITHIN

Although life around us exemplifies the combination of the elements, we separate these out in ritual and magic to symbolize and honor the sacred life-force that forms all of existence. Symbolism is a key principle of Wiccan spirituality and magical tradition. In a culture where rationality rules, sometimes we need to bypass our conscious, sensible, rational selves by appealing to our instinctive selves, in order to tap into the deep spiritual well within. This deep level is the divine within us, the umbilical by which we are joined to the sum of the divine, the Goddess. The instinctive self responds to symbols, and these are the gateway to the world of the "semiotic" or "Goddess space," the primordial space-time of spirit and magic. Accordingly, when witches work ritual and magic in sacred space, we symbolize the elemental aspects of the material Universe in order to draw upon them in the transformational work we are undertaking.

the symbolism of the elements

Element	Direction	Color	Associated human trait
Air	East	Yellow	Rational thought
Fire	South	Red	Willpower, courage
Water	West	Blue	Emotions
Earth	North	Green	Physicality
Spirit	Center	Purple or white	

For witches, the symbolism of the five elements, the fundamental stuff of life itself, is of primary importance.

Whenever witches work in sacred space (see pages 186-217) we invoke the elements, asking them to bring their gifts and energies to support our magical work. We set Air, Fire, Water and Earth in the four sacred directions; the cardinal points of the compass—east, south, west and north respectively—with Spirit at the centre of the circle.

It is important to remember that the elements are a physical reality, as well as part of a magical and spiritual system of symbols. Their physical manifestation is the very basis of spiritual and magical work. We breathe Air and its movement carries plant spores and aids pollination, as do the birds that wing through it. Fire is the warmth and light of the Sun, without which there would be no life on this planet. Water covers over three-fifths of the Earth's surface and our evolutionary ancestors crawled out from it onto dry land. Earth is rock, stone, soil, the nourishment of the vegetation that it supports. Spirit is in the life-giving connections we see all around us, much in the way that we perceive the effects of love, but never its separate, physical essence; it is the most mysterious and wonderful of the elements.

For witches, the five elements are the basis of all existence. We express their sacred nature in the sign of the pentacle, the upright five-pointed star in a circle. Within this symbol, the elements of Air, Fire, Water, Earth and Spirit are joined by one single unbroken line, encompassed by the sacred circle of life that has no beginning and no ending. The very fact that so many witches wear the pentacle as a sign of pagan spirituality demonstrates the importance with which the elements are regarded within the Craft.

Water covers most of our planet's surface.

Air

COMMUNICATION, REASON AND MEMORY

In sacred space, the eastern segment for this element is often decorated in yellow, with wind-chimes, feathers, carved birds, airborne seeds, scented herbs such as lavender or mint, and wands. It may include symbols or depictions of deities we associate with Air: Athena, goddess of wisdom; or Hermes (Mercury), god of swiftness and communication. We burn incense at this quarter of the sacred circle, as Air is the element of scent. When we invoke Air, we are not merely invoking an element external to ourselves, but one that resides

WORKING WITH AIR

1 Set aside some time alone to focus on your breath. Relax and slow your breathing. Take a deep breath into your lungs through your nostrils, hold for as long as is comfortable and expel through your mouth. Repeat three times.

2 Imagine the next breath is your first ever; hold and as you breathe out, imagine it is your last. How does it feel? Try to remember a time when your breathing was impeded, perhaps by a cold. What did this feel like?

3 Take a deep breath and make a moaning sound as you breathe out, changing the sound by the shape of your mouth, constricting your throat, positioning your tongue. Now try to form word-sounds without expelling breath. What happens when you do this?

4 Take a walk on a windy day. How does the speed and power of the air's movement affect the landscape around you? What do you hear, smell and feel?

within us. It is important, therefore, to work toward building a relationship with Air at a physical as well as a symbolic level.

The symbolic functions of Air are concerned with reason, learning, intellectual knowledge, communication, the law, movement, expedition and language. The physical gifts of Air are breath, the wind, sound, scent and memory. Collect symbols that encapsulate the element of Air and work with Air through your breath-work, meditating on your chosen symbols and conscious contact with Air in the natural world.

RITUAL WELCOME TO AIR

[Officer for Air]: *In the east, the element of Air; communication, reason and memory, our first breath and our last, you are honored in this circle. Be present at our rites and bring to this circle your gifts of clarity, teaching, learning and understanding.*

[Officer lights a yellow candle in the east]: *Hail and welcome!*

[All]: *Hail and welcome!*

Ritual staffs and wands symbolize Air.

fire
INSPIRATION, PASSION AND COURAGE

In ritual space, the Fire quarter is often decorated in red, with candles, lamps, carved dragons or salamanders, flowers and associated herbs, spices and gums such as frankincense, cinnamon, cactus or coriander, and athames (witches' knives) or swords. Symbols or images of deities associated with Fire may be included: Brighid, Celtic fire goddess or Belenos, god of the Sun. We burn lamps and candles in the south of our circles as physical representations

Blades often represent Fire.

working with fire

1 Walk through a park or town on a sunny day. Become conscious of the warmth of the Sun on your face, and the light that penetrates your closed eyelids.

2 How are the people, animals or plants around you affected by the light and heat of the Sun?

3 Another form of Fire is electricity. In mild weather, if you are at home alone, turn off all but strictly essential sources of electricity for one evening. Spend the evening in candlelight, without TV or music. If you can, light a bonfire outside.

4 How does the lack of electricity affect your activities? What do you experience with the different forms of fire you are using to create light and heat?

RiTUAL welcome TO Fire

[Officer for Fire]: *In the south, the element of Fire; inspiration, passion and courage, the spark that ignited our existence, you are honored in this circle. Be present at our rites and bring to this circle your gifts of willpower, daring and creativity.*

[Officer lights a red candle in the south]: *Hail and welcome!*

[All]: *Hail and welcome!*

Lamps symbolize light as a gift of Fire.

of Fire. In order to summon our inner Fire, we need to connect with and understand its function in the physical Universe as well as within Wiccan symbolism. This requires a little time set aside to consider the element in all its aspects and to experience its material function in our own lives.

The symbolic functions of Fire are inspiration, willpower, courage, activity and energy, and empowerment. The physical gifts of Fire are flame, combustion, electricity, warmth and light, body-heat and the rays of the Sun. Assemble some symbols that represent Fire and continue working with it through your conscious contact with its various forms in everyday life, and by meditating on your chosen symbols.

Water
INTUITION, DREAMS AND EMOTIONS

In our rituals, the Water quarter is often decorated in blue, with glass pebbles, depictions of sea-creatures, watery herbs and flowers such as roses, hyacinths, myrtle and lovage, and a chalice. We may add symbols or images of Water-associated deities, such as Rhiannon, Welsh goddess of rebirth, or Yemana, Santeria goddess of the sea. Working with the element of Water involves having direct knowledge of the vital purpose it serves in our physical environment as well as understanding its symbolic nature and meaning. In order to connect with Water, set aside time to find out more about it and experience for yourself its physical impact on our daily lives.

WORKING WITH WATER

1 Go to a beach or shore of a tidal sea, river or lake, and walk along the edge of the water at low tide. Walk with your eyes cast down toward the ground.

2 What do you see? How has the water affected its form? Observe the humans on the shore. What are they doing? Where are they looking? What attracts humans to watersides?

3 Research your local tides in the library or on the internet.

4 Set aside time to meditate; close your eyes and place the index finger of your left hand on the bone on the inside of your right wrist on your pulse. How does it feel to know that you carry rivers, streams and tributaries inside you? What function do streams and rivers serve on our planet?

The spiritual significance of Water is balance, healing, love and the emotions, mystery, birth, women's cycles and arcane knowledge. Its physical gifts are cleansing, life-giving moisture, cooling, quenching and the blood and fluids of our bodies. In order to continue your work with Water, gather and meditate on symbols that represent this element, and build a more conscious awareness of Water's everyday physical functions.

Rivers and streams are the arteries of the planet.

In the circle the chalice is the symbol for Water.

RITUAL WELCOME TO WATER

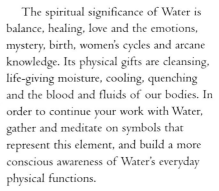

[Officer for Water]: *In the west, the element of Water; intuition, dreams and emotions, seas, rain, rivers and the primordial waters of birth, you are honored in this circle. Be present at our rites and bring to this circle your gifts of love, balance and healing.*

[Officer lights a blue candle in the west]: *Hail and welcome!*

[All]: *Hail and welcome!*

earth
FERTILITY, STABILITY AND PRACTICALITY

In Wicca, the Earth quarter is usually decorated in green, and contains living plants, wood, crystals and stones, fallen branches and images of forest creatures, earthy herbs, gums and oils such as patchouli, cypress, yew or mandrake, and a pentacle. We may include images of appropriate deities such as Demeter, the harvest goddess or the Green Man.

The element of Earth—matter—is the basis of the physical Universe. Working with Earth requires an understanding of its physical nature and experience of the importance of "matter" on our planet, in our Universe and

working with earth

1 Set aside some time to go out into a local natural landscape. What shapes it and which species of plants and animals make their homes there? While you move, become conscious of the different textures that the surface of the ground yields.

2 Meditate on your own "earthliness." Close your eyes, and sitting or standing on the ground's surface, imagine yourself melding to the floor, becoming one with the

deep layers of soil, rock, roots and bones that extend beneath you.

3 Now rise and keep within yourself the image of your Earth-form. You are a moving mountain. How does that feel?

4 Touch the outline of your own body, a mountain range physically separate from but interdependent on the Earth. Have you thought of your Earth connection in such a way before?

Mountains are the bones of the planet.

our lives. Its presence is most obvious to us in the spectacular side of nature; in mountain ranges and canyons, earthquakes or erupting volcanoes. But it is evident in less dramatic ways, in our everyday experience. It forms the matter and bones of our own bodies, the ground on which we walk, and feeds the vegetation that keeps our planet green and living.

The spiritual properties of Earth are manifestation, fruition, fertility, embodiment and solidity. Its physical gifts are sensation, physicality, food, shelter and the shield of protection. Build your connection with Earth by continuing to experience and meditate on its physical properties and gather symbols that represent its physical and spiritual gifts.

RITUAL WELCOME TO EARTH

[Officer for Earth]: *In the north, the element of Earth; fertility, stability and practicality, rock, crystal, soil, bones and body, you are honored in this circle. Be present at our rites and bring to this circle your gifts of sheltered protection and manifestation.*

[Officer lights a green candle in the north]: *Hail and welcome!*

[All]: *Hail and welcome!*

Spirit
CONNECTION, MAGIC, AND TRANSFORMATION

Called Ether in some Wiccan traditions, Spirit is set in the center of the ritual space which we decorate in purple or white. We use spider and web symbols and totems denoting divine magical patrons such as Hecate or Changing Woman, and decorate with quartz crystals, threads and distaffs. Working with the element of Spirit requires an understanding of its

Spirit is sometimes represented in the circle by crystals.

function within our everyday lives, which calls for imagination and a willingness to set aside preconceived ideas.

Spirit—connection—is the soul of formation and interdependence. Because it weaves irrevocable change, it is often expressed as *trans-formation*. As with love or courage, we recognize its effects rather than a separate, physical presence. Spirit oversees and takes part in the birth and death of stars. It is present in our everyday existence, joining Earth to sky, cobweb to tree and

WORKING WITH SPIRIT

1 Consider the connections in your own life. Calculate how many people you come into personal contact with in an average week. On that basis, assess the number they come into contact with.

2 Continue radiating outward to further contact generations. What does this tell you about the impact we have on others on a daily basis?

3 Think about the air we breathe in a similar way; also the heat we create, the water cycle, the genetic material we humans share.

Ritual Welcome to Spirit

[Officer for Spirit]: *In the center, the element of Spirit; connection and magic, weaver and web, you are honored in this circle. Be present at our rites and bring to this circle your gifts of transformation.*

[Officer lights a purple or white candle in the center]: *Hail and welcome!*

[All]: *Hail and welcome!*

Spirit is the element of transformation.

people to one another. When we look at a web we see the thread and the woven pattern, but which part of it, physically, is connection? What we perceive as connections are actually threads that have been placed in a particular way. Connection itself does not have a separate physical presence outside of the web's shaping. Thus it is with Spirit.

The element of Spirit represents transformation. When you are ready to step onto the spiritual path of Wicca, ask Spirit to reveal a connection, a truth, a way forward. Be patient and your answer will come. Collect your own Spirit symbols and nurture your own Spirit by meditating on them often.

PATHS AND TRADITIONS

The many traditions

Just as Wicca comes under the umbrella of paganism, Wicca itself is an umbrella term that shelters a number of distinctive flavors of witchcraft. It is a veritable rainbow of traditions, each with their own history, terms of reference and modes of organization. For some, the focus of their "difference" may be the fact that they follow a particular initiatory system or a particular approach or methodology used in their rites. For other traditions, the key differences from other groups may be concentrated in more overtly political issues, such as approaches to gender and sexuality.

The diversity found within Wicca is considered to be a positive strength by those wise enough to understand why such differences exist. Part of the reason that the Craft can accommodate stylistic and political dissimilarities between traditions is that the differences invariably reinforce the similarities between them; we all follow an organic, nature-based religion that pre-dates written history, even if we have organized the way we practice more recently. We also practice magic and many of the traditions borrow and learn from each other's various customs, methods and ingredients of spells and spell-work.

DIVERSITY

Wicca does have the occasional "purist" who will insist that the circle has to be cast in a particular way, or that one must have been initiated by a high priest or priestess of the opposite sex (usually because their tradition practices gender polarity), and even those who are rather disparaging about the practices of others; every religion has them. However, for every professed Wiccan who displays intolerance, there are thousands who are open-minded

about other people's choices and recognize, being truly wise, the importance of diversity rather than conformity.

The following descriptions of the different paths and various affinities of groups and solo workers are indicative rather than definitive. If you want to learn more about a particular tradition, there is a plethora of resources in libraries, bookshops and on the internet to explore further. I have included a brief reference to groups that are non-Wiccan, mainly because witches often find themselves rubbing shoulders with them. If you should find that your own practices cross over into different traditions, don't worry; most witches come under the eclectic grouping!

Witchcraft is a diverse path with many traditions.

Different paths

The roots of modern Wicca are found all over Europe and the near East, in the spiritual focus of our ancestors and in strands of paganism that have withstood the buffeting of time by disguising themselves as folklore and country wisdom. The story of modern Wicca's awakening, however, is far more recent and began in England in 1951 with the repeal of the 1736 Witchcraft Act, subsequently replaced by the Fraudulent Mediums Act. The impetus for its

The roots of Wicca are both recent and ancient.

repeal was its employment in the prosecution in 1944 of a spiritualist medium Helen Duncan, who attracted the attention of the naval authorities by revealing to members of the public the sinking of ships whose details had not yet been publicly released. The fact that the Act was still on the statute books incensed a number of public figures, who were concerned that its existence was a slur on the reputation of British law, and consequently it was repealed.

The Act's repeal effectively legalized witchcraft in England and enabled the publication of works describing the practices of covens.

FOUNDER OF MODERN WICCA

Gerald Gardner, recognized as the founder of modern Wicca, had already published in 1949 a fictional work titled *High Magic's Aid*. However, with the repeal of the Witchcraft Act and the death of his high priestess Old Dorothy Clutterbuck in that same year, he was free to write a nonfictional account of Wicca: *Witchcraft Today*, published in 1954. Although much of Gardner's work was based on the practices of covens operating in the early twentieth century and borrowed heavily from ancient esoteric documentation, he was also influenced by the work of some of his contemporaries, and included some flourishes of his own.

Debates about Gardner's *Book of Shadows*—the recorded litany, customs, spells and rituals of a witch—continue. Most people now credit his high priestess Doreen Valiente with the emphasis given to the Goddess. She is also the author of the *Mother Charge*, the words of the Goddess to her people, with which many Wiccan groups still open their Esbats or Full Moon celebrations. However, Gardner's contribution was seminal to the development of modern Wicca and since its early foundation it has grown to encompass a whole range of approaches and traditions.

The following are examples of some of the key expressions of the many different styles and flavors of Wicca, but remember that a paragraph cannot possibly encapsulate the meaning of a tradition which has its own influences, history and customs. If you want to learn more, you will need to do some research or better still, talk to a practicing member of that tradition to learn more about it.

GARDNERIAN WICCA

Named for Gerald Gardner, this tradition enfolds elements of ancient traditions and, because of its local origins, the folklore and customs of English paganism. It uses the basic pattern of a ritual circle, and elemental quarters for Air, Fire, Earth and Water, though the color symbolism differs from most other Wiccan traditions in that the color for Air is blue, for Earth, brown or black and for Water, green.

Gardnerians tend not to emphasize the element of Spirit.

Gardnerian Wicca venerates the Horned God of the Greenwood and the Goddess of Nature. Generally, Gardnerian Wicca is celebrated while "sky-clad"—naked. A high priest and high priestess lead each coven, with emphasis on the leadership of the high priestess. The Gardnerian system marks spiritual progress by a series of initiatory rites and is based on gender bi-polarity, which means that all things are divided into masculine/feminine opposites.

All paths of Wicca have a nature-orientation.

ALEXANDRIAN WICCA

This form of Wicca developed out of the Gardnerian system in the 1960s and is named for Alex Sanders, who with his partner Maxine developed a tradition that incorporated elements of Judeo-Christian sources, as well as aspects of the Greek and Egyptian mysteries and Celtic traditions.

Alexandrians honor the triple Goddess in all her aspects (maiden, mother and crone) and dual God (dark and light)—though some practitioners are also eclectic in their approach to deities. Alexandrian Wicca uses the basic framework set down by Gardnerian Wicca, but honors five sacred elements and uses the now widely recognized color symbolism set out on pages 78.

SAXON WICCA

Saex-Wicca was formulated by Raymond Buckland in the early 1970s. He is also accredited with introducing Wicca to the USA. Saex-Wicca is based on the

Gardnerian framework, but draws in aspects of English Saxon and Scots Pictish traditions.

HEDGEWITCHES AND SOLITARIES

The traditions outlined above are generally practiced in groups, but in Wicca there are many witches who practice on their own. The accurate title of this group is Solitaries, and they may practice any tradition of Wicca; what sets them apart is that they work alone. Solo workers are sometimes called Hedgewitches, though strictly speaking Hedgewitchery is the work of a Wise-Woman or Cunning-Man serving a community, knowledgeable in the ways of nature, herbal magic and traditional healing. The niceties of distinction are not always observed, however, and some city witches are keen to use the term to emphasize the origins of their spiritual path.

HEREDITARY

In Wicca, a Hereditary is a witch who has inherited Craft knowledge through their own family, or initiation into an hereditary group. Since the practices of such groups will differ according to what has been passed on to them, it is almost impossible to pinpoint what any particular Hereditary practices.

RADICAL FAIRY/DIANIC WICCA/RECLAIMING TRADITION

In theory there is no reason why Wicca should not be socially inclusive, but unfortunately some individuals or groups use, for example, gender bipolarity to justify their own homophobia or sexism. Consequently, some witches have worked to create positive spiritual space for women, bisexuals, lesbians and gay men. The Radical Fairy tradition was created by and for gay men, and in some groups there is an emphasis on the God Dionysus.

Most Dianic groups are either exclusively lesbian or female, and as their name suggests, the Goddess Diana is their chief patron. The Reclaiming Tradition, influenced by the work of Starhawk and Macha M. Nightmare, is inclusive, politically active and outspoken on issues of all forms of social discrimination. They operate on a non-hierarchical basis, organize public rituals and camps, and are the "ecstatics" of the US movement, using trance and shamanistic methods in their practices.

ECLECTICISM

All witches are, to an extent, eclectic, but Eclectics are those who do not align themselves with any particular tradition and instead select, borrow, appropriate and redefine to suit their purpose, elements of other traditions. All done respectfully, of course!

All traditions of Wicca are branches of a natural, Earth-based religion.

PAGANISM

Wicca is a pagan religion, but not all pagans are witches. Sometimes described as "non-aligned," some venerate a god or goddess, while others honor divinity within nature (pantheism), without reference to a deity. Beyond that, the customs and practices vary enormously. Most follow the eight festivals of the solar year and mark the Moon's cycle.

DRUIDRY

Druids are the close Celtic pagan relatives of witches. They revere nature as divine, celebrate, generally the four major solar festivals, and honor a God or Goddess. They sometimes organize along initiatory and hierarchical lines, but not always. Like witches, Druids are male or female.

ASATRU AND THE NORTHERN TRADITION

Asatru, meaning "loyalty to the Aesir" (Norse gods), is a religion of Norse heathenism based on the surviving historical records of the Norse pagan religions. It stays close to the original religion of the Norse people, and in Scandinavia is called *Forn Sidr* or "Ancient Way." The origins of Asatru are genuinely ancient and in Iceland it has state recognition. Since the 1970s it has expanded rapidly in Scandinavia, northern Europe and North America. The Asatru do not, as a rule, describe themselves as Wiccan or witches, but the "northern" tradition of witchcraft draws on many of the same deities and traditions to which the Asatru hold true.

Different affinities

Not only does Wicca derive from a variety of traditions, but there are also differences in the deities that witches honor and celebrate. In some cases, the chosen tradition will be strongly associated with a particular pantheon. Established groups often have a patron deity, and a group of gods and goddesses to which they are dedicated, or favorites with whom they work. Some groups are openly eclectic and willingly embrace the god and goddess affinities that newcomers bring; others work exclusively with a group of deities. The same is true of individuals—some witches work exclusively with a particular pantheon while others are more "mix and match" in their approach.

Many witches refer to the ancestors of the land.

The most popular single-origin pantheons seem to be Celtic, Northern, Greek and Roman, and Egyptian. Celticism, however, is very popular in Europe, and witches honor Brighid, Belenos, Cerne/Herne, Rhiannon, and Arhianrhod. The Northern tradition reveres deities of northern Europe, in particular the Norse, and sometimes Anglo-Saxon deities—Odin/Woden, Thor, Freya, Loki and Frigga. The Greek and Roman deities are popular in Europe, perhaps because their mythologies are so familiar to us. Similarly, the nineteenth- and twentieth-century archeological discoveries in Egypt fascinated Europeans. Isis, the All-Mother, is now one of the most beloved and best-recognized goddesses of contemporary Wicca. Many of us are keen to revisit and review the roles of gods and goddesses of the older pantheons and to explore their relevance for the inheritants of the older traditions.

PANTHEON PROBLEMS

New witches sometimes express anxiety over whether one should "mix" pantheons, and some purists insist that this should never be done. Groups who believe they are venerating deities of a single-origin pantheon are often honoring gods and goddesses that have a variety of origins but happened to be logged by writers or folklorists at a particular point of that pantheon's development. This is true, for example, of the Greek pantheon. The creation of the Greek/Roman pantheon came during the Hellenistic period, and many of the deities were pre-established local functionary gods of different areas of Greece and Italy. The term *Celtic* actually describes links between numerous tribes spread over a wide geographical area over a huge time-span. A witch or coven honoring a particular pantheon is likely to be incorporating a number of deities that were never worshipped together by their original followers or understood as a group.

As long as you approach the deities with respect, educate yourself regarding the peoples with whom they originate, and do not claim to be who you are not, say, a Native American shaman when you are, in fact, a white American or European, it really doesn't matter. Respect is what matters.

Learning from different traditions requires respect for them.

GODS AND GODDESSES

The gods and goddesses of Wicca

One of the aspects of Wicca that fascinates newcomers, academics and theologians alike is the special relationship that Wicca has with its gods and goddesses. Wicca is polytheistic—has more than one god or goddess. Witches see divinity as imminent—within us—and are pantheistic, seeing divinity in nature. In addition, we speak of "the Goddess" and "the God" but see no contradiction in honoring many deities, each of whom we perceive as being both distinctive and separate *and*, at times, aspects of the Goddess or the God. For someone accustomed to thinking of divinity as being "out there" or "up there," male and authoritarian, Wicca's relationship with its deities may appear somewhat puzzling. Because many of us have grown up in a culture that is used to a different concept of God, it requires a change in thinking in order to grasp what is actually a very simple approach to the nature of the divine.

Witches understand that we, as humans, embody the God or the Goddess, and because we do, we are all sacred. Nature also embodies the deity. Because of this very intimate way of connecting with the God or Goddess, we do not see the deity as being "above," or in authority over us. Rather, we see the God or Goddess as a friend, a confidante, a sister, brother, lover, a parent, a part of ourselves who is wiser and kinder to us than we often allow ourselves to be, and a brave advisor who does not flinch to remind us of what is right, even when "right" is difficult for us.

We also see the God and Goddess as the Great Spirit, the healer, the weaver of the web of life, soul of all nature. Because of our emphasis on the interconnectedness of all things, seeing the divine as counselor and friend as well as midwife to stars and planets does not pose a problem. What witches tend not to do is to see the deity as interventionist in human affairs. Wars, starvation, cruelty and injustice are human inventions—we do not call upon the deity to end these overnight as we do not see the God or Goddess as a quick-fix deity who can intervene in human history and take the credit or the blame for what is wrong with the world. However, we can, and do, call upon them to give us the courage and energy to go out and make those changes for ourselves.

Witches often draw upon the energy and patronage of the God or Goddess in spiritual work and in magic. If, for example, we are experiencing harassment

in the workplace, once we have taken practical measures such as alerting personnel and/or our union, we may choose to perform a ritual for ourselves. This could be to help us find the courage we need to continue challenging bullying behavior, or achieve a sense of balance that will aid us until the issue is resolved. If we are looking for courage we may call upon Oya, a Yoruba deity who is known to be very fierce and a good ally in tricky situations. We would ask her to lend us some of her fiery courage and

Statue of Osiris, Egyptian god of regeneration, from the tomb of Psamtik III.

resolve in facing our enemy and insisting upon our rights. If we are looking for a sense of balance, we may call upon Rhiannon, patron of people wronged by those who abuse their power, and ask her to lend us perspective, keep balance and let fairness prevail.

In drawing upon different aspects of deity, we summon reserves of power that we have within. Because the gods and goddesses embody, as well as symbolize, the powers with which we associate them, we are accessing our own spiritual strength and theirs when we call upon them. The same is true of our magical work when we ask particular deities to witness and lend power to the spells we perform. If we are asking for love to come into our lives, we may light a candle to honor Aphrodite, goddess of love, or Angus, the Celtic love god, and invoke them to witness and empower our work. If we are working to banish bad habits or behavior or to bind a wrongdoer, we may light a candle for old Saturn, god of old age and discipline, or Hecate, dark goddess of magic, and invoke their aid in our task. For witches, calling upon gods and goddesses in spiritual and magical work is a mark of respect and devotion—it is part of the Craft and our religion to honor the deities in this way.

Sometimes, either through meditation work, frequent contact with a deity or because a natural affinity has arisen, some witches develop a close relationship with a particular deity. It may be that they decide to devote themselves to that deity and to honor that individual god or goddess in their work. For some, this will be a rewarding, lifelong relationship. However, this does not preclude acknowledgment of other deities, or stop one from referring to "the God and the Goddess." Sometimes witches will work closely with a particular deity in one phase of their lives, and find that they have developed an affinity with another deity as they enter a new stage of their life cycle. Some women, for example, will have a natural affinity with Demeter, the Earth Mother, when they are pregnant, nursing or in a nurturing role in relationship to children, and find that once this role diminishes, they relate more closely to a goddess of independence—for example, Artemis.

Sometimes the deity comes to fit the moment, and offers what we need rather than what we think we need or ask for. It is often the case that a god or goddess will keep cropping up in meditation or in dreams or that we notice their symbols and totems in everyday life, until our attention is caught. Witches know never to ignore such clear signals; we have something to learn from the deity who is "waving" to us, even if—especially if—we can't imagine why we need to work with them just at the moment! When first stepping onto the spiritual path of Wicca, it is a good thing to ask the deities for guidance and invite a patron god or goddess to take you under their wing initially. You will find guidance on a visualization to help you find a patron deity on pages 140–143.

Glossary of gods and goddesses

In the following pages you will find a brief glossary (arranged by origin) of the gods and goddesses with whom most witches are familiar. You will find that there are more goddesses than gods because more is generally known of pagan goddesses and their functions. There are references to origins, key symbols and relevant associations. The following notes are intended as a starting point rather than intimately detailed descriptions—any truly inclusive glossary would stretch from here to the Moon and back! If you work with any of these deities, further research and your own experience will round out the picture more fully.

GREEK AND ROMAN DEITIES

Apollo A son of Greek god Zeus, Apollo is god of the Sun, of poetry, music, and the arts. He is a deity of light and clarity, representing rational thought, truth and healing. One of his most famous sites was the Oracle at Delphi, where priestesses would breathe in the smoke of burning laurel leaves, enter a trance, then give predictions and offer insights to seekers visiting the shrine. Apollo's arrows—the rays of the Sun—strike us as inspiration and insight. His healing rays also offer solace to the sick or downhearted.

Origin: Greece.

Symbols and associations: *Sunburst, laurel leaves, arrows.*

Artemis/Diana Maiden goddess of the forest and the night sky, her bow is the waxing crescent of the Moon. As maiden she is independent, spirited, and is associated with women-only spaces. Once a goddess of childbirth through her lunar associations, nowadays she is more often seen as a goddess of independence, integrity and action, and an antidote to patriarchy. Patron of

Athena, goddess of wisdom and learning.

Dianic and other women-only circles and covens.
Origins: *Greece/Italy.*
Symbols and associations: *Waxing crescent moon, the bow, she-bears.*

Athena/Minerva Goddess of wisdom, communication, science, mathematics and the arts, and intellect. Athena is a patron of writers, and known to bestow the "Owl Gift"—the ability to write and communicate clearly—on those who honor her. Like Apollo, she is a deity of rational thought, clarity of purpose and planning. However, her story is much older and she is also a goddess of crafts such as weaving and of natural creativity. Thus she is a conduit for turning thought into action, and a catalyst for joining intellect with intuition. Athena is a protector and defender against the forces of unreason and brute destruction.
Origins: *Crete/Greece and Mycenae/Italy.*
Symbols and associations: *Upward pointing equilateral triangle, snakes, spirals, owl, weaving.*

Aphrodite/Venus Goddess of love and beauty, of sexuality and sensuality. Often pictured rising from the sea on a shell, Aphrodite is the epitome of female beauty and sexuality. Our sister planet Venus, sometimes our morning/evening star, is named for her Roman counterpart, reflecting the shining beauty associated with this goddess. Aphrodite rules the emotions, an extension of her link to the waters. In the mystic Qabalah, the sphere of Netzarch is ruled by Venus, and this is the domain of the lover, of erotic spirituality, creativity and art. Aphrodite is often invoked for love spells in Wicca.

Origins: Asia, Cyprus, Greece/Italy.

Symbols and associations: Rose, myrtle, scallop shell, water, Venus (planet), morning dew.

Aries/Mars God of action, defense and protection. In ancient times he was seen as the bringer of war and discord; nowadays, Aries (or Ares) is regarded by witches as a catalyst for change. There were some differences between the Greek and Roman deity, but both are celebrated in similar ways these days. With Aries's Roman counterpart giving his name to the red planet in our solar system, it is clear that Aries is seen as hot-headed and volatile. However, in ancient Rome, Mars was seen as a god of farming and of spring, as well as being a warlike entity, which invites contemporary Wiccans to review the way he has become a bit of an action-man figure!

Origins: Greece/Italy.

Symbols and associations: Mars (planet), the color red.

Demeter/Ceres Goddess of corn and seasonal growth. Demeter is an aspect of the Mother Goddess, and is also sometimes referred to as "Habundia," a Roman allegory for abundance. Demeter, as the mother of Persephone, mourns the disappearance of her daughter who has gone to stay with Hades in the world of the dead. As Demeter mourns the Earth's vegetation dies, and is only renewed when Persephone returns. As Persephone is destined to descend into Hades every six months, the seasonal cycle is repeated each year. Demeter is a loving mother and her relationship with Persephone is an encouraging symbol in a world where patriarchy often sours relationships between women. Contemporary Wiccans also see a source of inspiration for environmentalism in her renewal of the Earth.

Origins: Greece/Italy.

Symbols and associations: Cornucopia (horn of plenty).

Dionysus God of wine and ecstasy. Seen by many Wiccans as the twin archetype to Apollo, Dionysus is the god of divine madness, the ecstasy of spirit and body. His followers were known to go into frenzies during worship and experience trance and violently ecstatic states. Just as Apollo rules over the rational aspect of self, so Dionysus represents the side of us that is animal, intuitive, ecstatic and unruly. Because Dionysus is cut to pieces and resurrected, he is also associated with rebirth, renewal and the Underworld. In legend, he is a traveler and exile who is finally accepted as one of the twelve major Olympian gods. This history links him with the difficult paths of change and transformation, coming from initiation onto the path of spiritual and arcane knowledge.
Origins: Greece.
Symbols and associations: Grapes, vine-leaves, masks, dance.

Flora Goddess of spring, flowers and plants that bloom, Flora is an ancient Roman deity linked to the seasonal greening of the Earth. She is usually depicted with wreaths of flowers in her hair. A favorite of courtesans, Flora was also seen as a goddess of pleasure.
Origins: Italy.
Symbols and associations: Flower wreaths and hoops.

Gaia Primal mother goddess and name given to the Earth as a living being. Gaia gave birth parthenogenically to all existence, and is seen as generous and giving as well as in need of our protection in order to retain her fragile balance.
Origins: Greece.
Symbols and associations: Stones and crystals of the Earth, soil and greenery, trees.

Hecate Crone goddess of witches, magic, the night, and ruler of crossroads, borders and thresholds. Like Freya (see pages 126–127), Hecate is drawn through the sky in a chariot pulled by cats, though Hecate is also associated

Aries, god of action, and Aphrodite, goddess of love, from a fresco in Pompeii, Italy.

with other nocturnal creatures. She watches over travelers and those making major life-decisions. She is a weaver of wisdom and the midwife who guides us into life then from life to death. She is mistress of arcane knowledge, magical and herbal, and is associated with cauldrons and broomsticks—both accoutrements associated with witchcraft. Hecate is enormously popular with contemporary witches.

Origins: *Greece and southern Europe.*

Symbols and associations: *Cats, crossroads, cauldrons, broomsticks, bats, moths, ravens and crows, owls, bones, herbal knowledge, spiders and webs.*

Hephaestus/Vulcan/Wayland/Govennon Blacksmith/metal-working god. The ability to work with Earth, Air, Fire and Water in their primary forms to create objects of beauty and worth was considered sacred in the ancient world, and blacksmith gods were honored as wise alchemists and magicians. In the Celtic world, Wayland or Govennon had similar functions as smiths who transformed base elements into armor, horseshoes or jewelry. It is possible that all blacksmith gods are the remnants of much older, more primitive gods of creation and secret knowledge. They are all credited with the ability to transform and redefine base matter, and represent initiation into the mysteries and the quest for embodied spirituality.

Origins: Greece/Italy/Ireland/northern Europe.
Symbols and associations: Anvils, hammers, horseshoes, iron, metalwork, alchemy.

Hera/Juno Goddess of marriage, partnerships, the home. Seen sometimes as the consort of Olympian Zeus, Hera is a powerful goddess in her own right, a defender of hearth and home, partnerships and children. She is a family goddess in the truest sense of the word and a protector of the integrity of households and all their members. She is patron of parenthood, and wise counselor and protector of the young, and perhaps for that reason is often called upon to protect newborns.

Origins: Greece/Italy.
Symbols and associations: Peacock feathers, turquoise stones, loving cups.

Hermes/Mercury Messenger god of speed and communication. Hermes is seen as the very soul of swiftness and is often depicted in winged sandals, carrying a *caduseus*, a staff entwined with two snakes, which indicates that his messages are from the Gods. The caduseus is also a symbol of healing and health, with which Hermes is secondarily related. His primary symbolism, however, is that of communication and speed, and the planet nearest the Sun in our system is named for his Roman counterpart, reflecting his link with speediness. Hermes is associated with the ability to speak with wit and intelligence. In Greek legend, he is a trickster and thief, a bringer of dreams, patron of travelers, and a guide to souls on their way to the Underworld.

Origins: *Greece/Italy.*

Symbols and associations: *Caduceus, winged sandals/helmet, planet Mercury, color yellow, feathers.*

Hesta/Hestia/Vesta Goddess of the hearth-fire. Hesta is a protector of the hearth and oversees household tasks and crafts. In ancient Rome a retinue of unmarried girls and women were charged with keeping her flame burning. She is a goddess of integrity and protection, and guards the heart of any home where she is honored. Hesta is associated with cooking, warmth and heat, the boundaries of the home and crafts such as pottery and homemaking.

Origins: *Greece/Italy.*

Symbols and associations: *Hearth-fire, flames.*

Pan God of herds, fertility and male sexuality. Half-man, half-goat, Pan represents our most basic instincts. He is the embodiment of our animalistic natures and is very earthy. One of our most basic preservation instincts is the "fight or flight" surge of adrenaline that keeps us alive in crises; Pan lends his name to the basic primal fear that keeps this drive alive in us—panic. Popular with gay men's groups, Pan is affectionately known as "Old Horny"—an epithet he shares with Cernunnos (see pages 123–124).

Origins: *Greece/Italy.*

Symbols and associations: *Goatskins, horns.*

Persephone/Kore Maiden goddess of spring and the Underworld. Persephone is the daughter aspect of the Demeter/Persephone myth (see Demeter page

110), and is jointly queen of the dead and goddess of spring. This combination makes her an extraordinary figure of female autonomy. Her caring aspect is seen in her insistence on returning each year to Hades, the land of the dead. She is celebrated in spring and autumn.

Origins: *Greece.*

Symbols and associations: *Pomegranate, spring flowers.*

Pluto/Hades God of the Underworld, king of the dead. Sometimes a gloomy deity, he is also seen as something of a magician. The planet farthest from our Sun in our solar system is named for him, as it is in constant darkness.

Origins: *Greece.*

Symbols and associations: *The number eight, wand.*

Selene Moon goddess. Lady of the Full Moon, Selene is depicted as a beautiful woman with the Moon as her crown. She is ruler of tides, oversees women's cycles, reproduction, pregnancy and birth, and guards against delusions brought about by the severance of humans from natural cycles.

Origins: *Greece.*

Symbols and associations: *Full Moon.*

Uranus God of the heavens. Primal rain god who was born to Gaia parthenogenically. His rain made Gaia fruitful and she produced with him the Titans, among them Cronos, who overthrew Uranus, only to be overthrown himself by Zeus (see below). Primal male fertility deity.

Origins: *Greece.*

Symbols and associations: *Sickle, raindrops.*

Zeus/Jupiter/Jove Father and thunder god. Sometimes described as the ruler of the Hellenistic pantheon, Zeus is a father aspect of divinity. Known as the

Cloud Gatherer or Thunderer, he is honored as a god who knows how to get things done when all patience is worn out! He is a protector of freedom, patron of humanity, and advocate of those served with injustice. He is the soul of hospitality and generosity, and bringer of joy—hence the term *jovial*. He teaches us to share our good fortune—a god of charity and giving.

Origins: Greece/Italy.

Symbols and associations: Planet Jupiter, color purple, lightning fork, eagles.

EGYPTIAN DEITIES

Anubis Jackal-headed god associated with the Underworld. Anubis is responsible for weighing the souls of the dead when they enter the afterlife. He is a god of prophecy and divination, and knows the destiny of all mortals. Anubis is a deity associated with the magical arts and so beloved of Wiccans everywhere.

Origins: Egypt.

Symbols and associations: Scales, jackals, divination and magic.

Bast/Bastet Cat-headed goddess. Associated with music and dancing, Bast is also a goddess of joy and her devotees in the ancient Egyptian delta were believed to have honored her with enthusiastically licentious celebrations! All cats are sacred to Bast, and are seen as aspects of the Divine Female, so Bast is popular with contemporary cat-loving pagans and witches.

Origins: Egypt.

Symbols and associations: Cats.

Hathor Goddess of the Sun and bringer of rains. Associated with the inundation of the Nile in the desert kingdom of Egypt, Hathor is seen as a fertility as well as solar deity. She represents the Earth-sky connections that engender and maintain life, and is a goddess of light. Sometimes depicted wearing the solar disc between her cow horns, she is seen as a deity who leads us out of confusion into understanding.

Origins: *Egypt.*

Symbols and associations: *Solar disc between cow horns, turquoises.*

Horus Falcon-headed God. Horus has many aspects, including those of a sky God; he is a god of the horizon, of day and night, dusk and dawn. His eye is said to bring protection against evil and is a symbol used in spell-work today. Child of the Isis, the All-Mother and goddess of magic and transformation, Horus has the power of protective magic. As a baby, he is seen feeding at his divine mother's breast, an image that spread all over North Africa and Europe via the Roman Empire, and is seen by some as the template for the later depictions of the Madonna and child of the Christian religion.

Origins: *Egypt.*

Symbols and associations: *Falcons, Eye of Horus, Sun and Moon.*

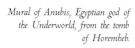

Mural of Anubis, Egyptian god of the Underworld, from the tomb of Horemheb.

Isis the All Mother, detail from tomb.

Isis Mother Goddess of all. The lover/sister of Osiris, Isis restores him to life after he has been cut to pieces by jealous Set and conceives of him the god Horus. Her association with restoration from the dead makes Isis a powerful magician and healer. She represents fertility and depictions of her feeding the infant Horus show her as nurturing mother. Isis is credited with the creation of written language, indicating that in the ancient world goddesses were not linked solely with fertility and reproduction. Isis is goddess of the Milky Way, said to be created from her breast-milk.

Origins: Egypt, North Africa.

Symbols and associations: Lapiz lazuli, blue agate, throne, Full Moon between crescent horns, falcon wings, stars.

Nephthys Goddess of magic and secret knowledge. Nephthys is a beloved sister of Isis and contemporary witches call on her to empower them with arcane knowledge and the skills with which to activate our innate magical powers. She is a goddess of sisterhood, darkness, childbirth and nursing. She is also a goddess of secrecy. Her magician status makes her particularly popular with witches.
Origins: Egypt.
Symbols and associations: Kite (bird).

Nut Goddess of the night sky. Nut is a primal deity whose whole body forms the vault of the heavens. She is sometimes depicted as arching over the Earth, her body the blue of the sky and fire of the stars. A basic creation deity.
Origins: Egypt.
Symbols and associations: Astronomy, the night sky, stars.

Osiris God of regeneration. Osiris is credited with bringing all the trappings of civilization to Egypt, as well as being a deity of corn and wine, crafts and religion. Like his son Horus, he is a god of the rising and the setting Sun, and is associated with regeneration because he was cut to pieces by Set before being reassembled by his sister/lover Isis, with whom he conceived their falcon-headed son (see Isis and Horus above). Nowadays, Osiris retains many of his original aspects as god of life, death and regeneration.
Origins: Egypt.
Symbols and associations: Corn, vine leaves.

Sehkmet Lion-headed goddess. Destroyer of disease and disposer of unwanted things, Sekhmet is a solar deity, closely associated with Bast. She is independent and fiery, and is called upon when there is heavy magical work to be done!
Origins: Egypt.
Symbols and associations: Lion-heads, sun discs.

Set God of the waning Moon, thunder and storms. He is an impatient, uncontrollable life-force, and in ancient times represented drought and destruction. Nowadays, his function is similar to that of Sekhmet, the necessary cutting away of surplus.

Origins: Egypt.

Symbols and associations: Waning Moon, lightning fork.

Thoth God of magic, wisdom, medicine, astronomy and writing, but especially of music. Said to have brought all magic and wisdom into being with the power of sound; Thoth is a great favorite with contemporary magicians who use incantation, drumming and song to invoke him. God of great knowledge.

Origins: Egypt.

Symbols and associations: Crescent Moon, the Eye of Ra (the Sun).

CELTIC AND NORTHERN EUROPEAN DEITIES

Angus/Oengus Celtic god of love and youth. Unusually a male representation of love and beauty. His music draws lovers of music and beauty to him. His kisses were said to turn into singing birds.

Origins: Ireland/Scotland.

Symbols and associations: Harp, songbirds.

Arhianrhod Goddess of "the Silver Wheel," the Moon and the stars. In Welsh mythology, the constellation *Corona Borealis* is known as "Caer Arhianrhod," the tower or castle of Arhianrhod. Connected with spinning and weaving, Arhianrhod is a goddess of connections, particularly those between birth, death and regeneration. She is a wisdom figure who keeps the knowledge of the past, the present and the future in her crystal tower. She represents deep soul knowledge, intuition and the mysteries of the life cycle.

Origin: *Wales.*
Symbols and associations: *Spinning wheel, webs, the Full Moon, stars.*

Belenos/Bel The Celtic Sun god dubbed "the British Apollo" by the Romans. Deity of light, health and healing, Belenos was thought—in some parts of northern Europe—to drive a chariot carrying the Sun's disc. In his healing aspect, he is associated with healing waters, wells and springs. The prefix *Bel* means "shining" and was often linked with solar and aquatic deities, such as the Romano-British goddess Belisama (shining one), so it is unsurprising that his image is found carved into the first-century BCE temple at Aqua Sulis, a natural spa in Bath, England. His name is given to the May festival of Beltane, which means literally "the fire of the God Bel," and part of the seasonal festival celebrating the rise of the Sun. His victory over the hours of darkness is celebrated at Litha, the summer solstice, and his imminent fall is marked by the sending of fiery wheels down hillsides at that time of year.
Origins: *Northern Europe, Britain.*
Symbols and associations: *Wheel, sunburst, head with penumbra or halo.*

Bel/Beli/Sol The female aspect of Bel/Belenos (see above), Bel or Beli is celebrated as a goddess in feminist and goddess-centred Wicca, and has many of the aspects attributed to her male counterpart. However, Bel is also seen as the inner, as well as the outer, physical Sun, and a link between the healing, regenerative power of the Sun and the nurturing, restorative power of the soul.
Origins: *Northern Europe, Britain.*
Symbols and associations: *Tidal rivers, the wheel, sunbursts, serpentine hair, May Day morning dew.*

Brighid/Bridie/Brigit Celtic fire goddess associated with healing, poetry and metalwork. The triple goddess Brighid has close connections with the Sun and her fire aspect is seen as the warming breath that warms the Earth to end winter and bring the thaw and the first snowdrops. Brighid is midwife to the spring, and is a protector of women, children and newborn animals, particularly sheep and cattle. Many healing shrines, wells and springs in England and Ireland are named for her. She is associated with serpents—ancient symbol of the healing powers of the Earth Goddess—and her festival is at Imbolc (or Oimelc), a time associated with the birth of lambs. Today Brighid is a goddess of independence, integrity and energy, often depicted in her threefold aspect with fiery red hair.

Origins: Ireland, Scotland, Isle of Man, England.

Symbols and associations: Fire, wells, healing cauldron, serpents, anvil and hammer, dandelion, snowdrops, amethysts, white candles.

Bloddueuth Maiden goddess of springtime and flowers. A "Green Woman" for the late spring, Bloddueuth in Welsh legends is built from flowers by a magician to provide a wife for the divine hero, Llew Llaw Gyffes, son of Arhianrhod. In this legend, Bloddueuth is portrayed as deceitful and is turned into an owl as punishment. Present-day pagans interpret this story slightly differently, seeing Bloddueuth's dual nature as spirit of Sun and Moon, as an aspect of the goddess involved in the initiation of the hero. Further, goddess-centred pagans

Herne leading the Wild Hunt in Richmond Park, England.

concentrate on her function as promoting vegetation and growth, and celebrate her at Beltane and in the early summer months.

Origins: *Wales.*

Symbols and associations: *Flower hoops, owls.*

Ceridwen Cthonic deity, also goddess of Earth wisdom. Sometimes seen as a crone aspect of the Goddess, she is also a mother and gives birth to Taliesin (Shining Brow), the great poet and bard. She initiates him through their famous shape-shifting chase, in which she finally swallows him as a corn of grain by turning herself into a hen and giving birth to him nine months later. Ceridwen is goddess of the cauldron of Earth, and regeneration. As shape-shifter, life-giver, initiator and mistress of magic, Ceridwen is a favorite goddess of modern-day Wiccans.

Origins: *Wales.*

Symbols and associations: *Cauldron, sows, hens, magic and shape-shifting.*

Cerne/Cernunnos/Herne Celtic antlered god and spirit of the Greenwood. Consort to the Mother Goddess and archetypal symbol of fertility and regeneration. Sometimes depicted as the Green Man, Jack-in-the-Green or Robin Hood, he is a favorite of contemporary Wiccans who see him as a positive male role model; a "green man" who cares for the environment, is capable of cyclical change and is a protector in touch with his emotions! Although his origins are truly ancient, he is seen as a virile young god and a wise, mature and knowing male aspect of the divine. Sometimes known as "Herne the Hunter," his divine status is sometimes confused with a mortal identity, as there appear to be many "last resting places" of Herne all over England; an echo, perhaps, of the rites recorded in very old folk songs where humans could take on the role of the fertility god by the "wearing of the horns" or antlers at Beltane. This god is very popular and particularly beloved in the contemporary Wiccan movement.

Origins: England.
Symbols and associations: *Green Man masks, the ram-headed serpent, antlers, the oak tree, acorns and oak leaves.*

Dagda Irish god known also as "the Dagda," or "Good God." He is seen as a primal father god, associated with the Earth and its seasons, as well as having both life-giving and death-dealing functions. His heavily symbolic club could slay and restore warriors to life, indicating an ancient aspect of life, death and regeneration. He is said to mate with Morrigan, the Irish goddess of death, ravens and the battlefield (see Morrigan, pages 127–128) once a year at Samhain, while she straddles a river. Not heavy on intellect, the Dagda is the embodiment of natural life cycles and urges, and the cycles of life and death. He is seen as a humorous figure, indicating that our pagan ancestors appreciated some of the absurdities of sexuality and our natural functions and appetites.
Origins: Ireland.
Symbols and associations: *Giant "club."*

Danu/Anu/Aine Irish Mother Goddess, mother of the *Tuatha de Danann*, the mysterious semi-divine race known as "Children of the Goddess." Ancient goddess of the land, of crops and natural greenery, her followers carried torches after dark through the fields and around hillsides with which she was associated, in order to bring Danu's blessings upon the Earth. She is a fertile goddess of agriculture, as well as protector against nightmares and fears. She is closely associated with Anu/Aine, a goddess with similar attributes who is also associated with the phases of the Moon and nurture. Some hills in Ireland are named the "Paps of Danu." This ties in with Danu's fertility and nurturing aspects, and her status as ancient Mother Goddess.
Origins: Ireland.
Symbols and associations: *Flaming torch, hillsides.*

The Norse goddess Freya, in her chariot that is drawn by cats.

Dis/Dispater Ancient primal father god of the Gauls. Originally a god of the Underworld, he later merged with aspects of Cernunnos (see pages 123–124) to become a fertility god, from whom the Gauls believed they all descended. Dis retained his function as ruler of the dead and of the Underworld, marking him as a god of fertility and rebirth, ruler over the mysteries of the womb and the grave.

Origins: Ancient Gaul (France).
Symbols and associations: Silver three-legged wheel or triskele.

Eostre/Ostara Fertility goddess associated with the spring equinox. Eostre is a deity of Teutonic/Germanic origin associated with conception and birth. She is linked with the fertility of humans, animals and crops as well as the natural vegetation of the Earth. Her totem is the hare, archetypal symbol of fertility and fecundity, and the egg, which is life in potential. She is an Earth and Moon goddess, linked to reproductive cycles and the wealth of the Earth. Her name is given to the festival of Easter which in the Christian calendar commemorates the rebirth of the fallen man-God, as well as to the pagan festival Eostre or Ostara which marks the vernal equinox.

Origins: *Northern Europe.*

Symbols and associations: *Hares, eggs, spring flowers and buds.*

A bronze statuette of the Norse thunder god, Thor, that was found in Iceland.

Epona/Rhiannon Horse goddess, sometimes portrayed as, or riding on, a mare. Epona is a goddess of travel and movement and represents our own links with the animal kingdom. She is also a deity of speed and change. Originally worshipped by the Gauls, Epona found devotees among the Roman legionnaires who, at the time of the invasion of Gaul, were impressed by Celtic horsemanship and the respect with which horses were treated. Epona is often linked with the Welsh deity Rhiannon, who also has an association with horses but who, in addition, is associated with the sea and is a goddess of natural justice and retribution.

Origins: *Northern Europe/Wales.*

Symbols and associations: *Horses, springtime, the sea, travel.*

Freya Goddess of love and sexuality. Also patron of *seidr* or "seeing," a practice of the Wise. Freya is transported in a chariot drawn by cats and she wears a necklace thought to be a yonic symbol, representing the source of all life. She is goddess of female sexuality and also an Earth deity of fertility and growth. Libations are poured at the hearth and onto the Earth to honor her.

Origins: *Northern Europe.*

Symbols and associations: *Necklaces, cats.*

Lugh Sun god. Lugh is a master of arts and crafts, a god of health and healing. His radiant aspect makes him a god of truth and clarity. He was a much beloved god of the Celtic world, and is today celebrated as patron of youth, virility and health.

Origin: *Ireland, Northern Europe.*

Symbols and associations: *Sunbursts, head with penumbra.*

Macha Goddess associated with horses and speed. She is an independent-spirited goddess, quick to take retribution on wrong-doers and sometimes bringer of dreams (nightmare). Associated with lightning, thunder and rain, Macha is good to have on your side if you have been wronged. She is a fierce protector of women in pregnancy and childbirth.

Origins: *Ireland.*

Symbols and associations: *Lightning fork, horses.*

Maeve/Mebh Goddess of female sexuality, sovereignty and self-determination. Maeve is a lively Irish goddess reputed to bed 30 men a day in order to be sexually satisfied; a positive, if somewhat raunchy, representation of female autonomy.

Origins: *Ireland.*

Symbols and associations: *May-blossom.*

Morrigan Raven goddess. Seen as a highly sexualized aspect of the Dark Mother, the Morrigan is goddess of the dark time of year and mates with the Dagda at

Samhain. Nowadays, the Morrigan is invoked to bring basic wisdom out of primal chaos and darkness—seen as positive potential—the place of creativity.

The Norse god Odin, shown with his crows Hugin (thought) and Munin (memory), from a manuscript in the Royal Library, Denmark.

Origins: Ireland.

Symbols and associations: Ravens, crows, bones.

Nuada Sun god. Nuada of the Silver Arm is a solar deity whose legend portrays him as a great king and hero. He is a god of protection and defense, and carries many of the usual qualities of a solar deity—healing, light, regeneration.

Origins: Ireland.

Symbols and associations: Silver sunburst.

Odin/Woden Norse/Saxon All-Father. Odin is a god of great knowledge. He possesses the secrets of the runes—a system of magical symbols—which he came by with great suffering. His legend tells that he had to hang upside down from a tree for nine days and nights in order to learn the secrets of the sacred runes, and he is attributed with bringing that knowledge to humankind by way of offering guidance to right living and spiritual growth. He rules over life and receives after death those who have lived with honor. He is a god of magic and oversees the connections between Earth and Sky.

Origins: Scandinavia.

Symbols and associations: Oak trees.

Thor Thunder god. Powerful champion of humankind, called upon when great strength is needed for a just cause. Thor is seen as good-humored, though he can be quick-tempered when injustice is involved.

Origins: Scandinavia.

Symbols and associations: Thunder, silver hammers.

Hugin

Odinn

Mini

þetta kynnd Cont
rasey. Þargar ða
ðu ríoðer. áðúr
Þyrðba Imgá
Iney. Et Þní-
ðu Villa slöð-
sem er Oðins.
þy lœ te.

ASIAN, AFRICAN AND MIDDLE EASTERN DEITIES

Astarte/Ishtar Goddess of love and sexuality, female allurement and primal creatrix. Associated with the stars, Moon and Sun as well as the Earth, she is also an ancient mother goddess archetype, linking sexuality and reproduction, sensuality and spirituality. A goddess of dance and beauty, like Aphrodite associated with the planet Venus.
Origins: Asia.
Symbols and associations: Serpents, stars, the Milky Way.

Innanna Goddess of the heavens and the Underworld, Innanna is an independent and spirited figure. She is a Moon goddess as well as an Earth deity. Her adventures in the Underworld are similar to those of many gods and goddesses who undergo sacrifice in order to gain wisdom and knowledge (see Odin page 128). She also has links with goddesses who venture into the Underworld, such as Persephone (see pages 114–115) and Freya (see pages 126–127), causing the vegetation on Earth to die, restoring it on her return, in the myth of the seasonal cycle. She is celebrated as a mistress of life and death, a wise woman and a trickster.

Origins: Ancient Sumer, Asia.
Symbols and associations: Seven stars in a circle, the Moon.

Kali Goddess of dance, female energy. Kali is part of the primal life-force. She dances the dance of

Kali represents part of the primal life-force.

destruction—that is to say the chaos out of which life is produced—and cuts away that which is not strictly necessary. In Wicca she is seen as a necessary aspect of creation, a positive way of channeling righteous anger and putting energy to good use. She is a fierce protector and symbol of direct action in good causes.
Origins: *India.*
Symbols and associations: *Fire and dance, the wheel of creation.*

Lilith Owl-footed goddess of childbirth, integrity and resistance against tyranny. Lilith is the dark side of the Moon and represents aspects of femaleness often outlawed within patriarchy. She is a lunar deity who oversees women's monthly cycles, pregnancy and childbirth, and she protects newborns.
Origins: *North Africa.*
Symbols and associations: *Owls, disc of the half-Moon.*

Mithras God of light and resurrection. Although the cult of Mithras originated in Persia, he became particularly popular with Roman soldiers. Today, his rites are seen as a celebration of the redemptive and regenerative life force. Mithras is seen as a solar god and a god of vegetation. He links reason and intuition, and represents inner as well as outward illumination. Celebrated particularly at the solar festivals, his major festival is at the winter solstice, when he is reborn.
Origins: *Persia, Asia, Europe.*
Symbols and associations: *Sunbursts.*

Oya Goddess of storms, positive and protective action and defense. Oya is a fierce goddess, but good to have on your side if you are being threatened or bullied. She represents the basic instinct for self-protection and is not averse to bouncing back to wrongdoers the results of their own deeds.
Origins: *Africa.*
Symbols and associations: *Copper shield, color red.*

VISUALIZATION

The importance of visualization

Visualization is a crucial part of a witch's spiritual and magical tool-kit. The ability to hold in our mind's eye aspects of our inner, spiritual landscape or to imagine the intended outcome of a spell is an important part of self-development, spell-work and ritual.

Visualization is used routinely to encapsulate the intent of the actions we are undertaking, and to direct the energy we are raising toward its goal. In magical and spiritual work, clarity of intention is fundamental to the success of our work and visualization is part of craft discipline.

This technique also enhances our potential to receive growth-enhancing clues from our deep intuitive selves. Going on guided journeys of discovery to our inner, spiritual and emotional landscapes is particularly important to our development as spiritual beings, which is why it is so embedded in Wicca as a developmental tool and a means of communication with the deities. It enhances

Exploration of inner landscapes is part of visualization.

our ability to envisage routinely
during circle and spell-work,
certainly, but it also helps us to
discover the power we have within us.

The skill of visualization is easier
to acquire than most people imagine.
If you were a natural daydreamer as a
child, you may find it easy to slip
into visualization or "path-working,"
as it is sometimes known. Those of
us who are still quite adept at
drifting off into a world of our own
are actually good natural storytellers;
we tell ourselves stories that we play
out in our imaginations. But
everybody has the basic ability to
imagine. It simply requires a
conscious effort to reclaim our
imaginative faculties—particularly
those who were discouraged from
daydreaming at school or at home—
and this will come with practice.

Some of us are more visual
than others and can produce vivid
imagery inside our heads, while
others find it easier to focus on a
narrative pattern—a storyline with
causes and consequences, actions and
outcomes. It really doesn't matter

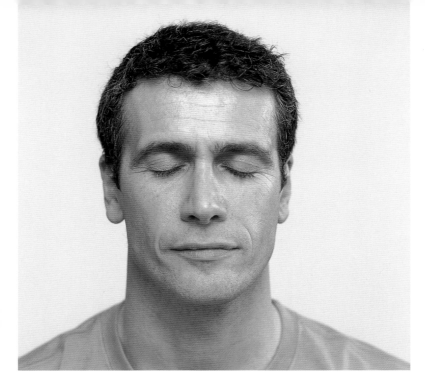

Guided visualization enables us to receive important messages from the inner self.

which type of imagining you use; it is more important that you learn to focus it to steer guided inner journeys, and develop the ability to receive and recognize the sometimes unexpected images and impressions that can emerge during the process.

Visualization is a form of meditation that deflects distracting thoughts of the everyday by providing a mental map of an inner journey. While the left-hand side of the brain is occupied with the story or map coordinates, the right-hand side of the brain—associated with random creativity, psychic abilities and magic—is free to become a transmitter and receiver. Important messages from the deep inner self, which is connected with the Whole, with Spirit, with the God or Goddess, may emerge during inner journeys.

Some people record a journey and play it back on tape so that they can concentrate on the journey itself. Others get a friend to read it aloud or, if in a group, nominate someone to guide everyone else through the visualization. It should be noted that recordings are not always successful, because tape recorders cannot adjust the speed of delivery to the needs of the person undertaking the journey. A whirring and clicking tape can also be quite distracting. Getting a friend to read out loud is a better option, but it requires some expertise on the part of the reader or guide, who needs to be aware of the appropriate speed at which to proceed, and the length of pauses involved. Facilitating visualizations sensitively is itself an acquired skill!

Over the following pages, you will find guidance for visualizations for a variety of purposes. If this is the first time you have attempted visualization, please read the preparatory information on pages 138–139. The best way to start, if you are working alone, is to read the visualization through at least three times, memorizing key aspects of the journey, then carry out the visualization from memory. You do not have to remember it word for word, just the main points. Keep a note pad and pen next to you so that you can record anything that strikes you as important as soon as you emerge from your inner journey. Just as we often forget dreams quickly after waking, the images, symbols and words given to us during visualizations fade like fairy gold in daylight unless we remember to write them down.

Preparation

When undertaking the following visualization exercises there are several things to bear in mind, particularly if you are a beginner. First, be patient with yourself; very few of us achieve spectacular results the first time we undertake a guided inner journey, and most of us drift off or lose concentration until we become more experienced. All that is needed is practice, patience and more practice!

You will need a quiet place where you will be undisturbed for the duration of your journey—up to 30 minutes. You also need to relax, concentrating on slowing your breathing, relaxing your muscles and finding a position in which you will be comfortable. Relaxed positioning is a prerequisite to any type of magical, spiritual or circle work, so it is a good idea to practice this.

Visualization work can take place indoors or outside.

how to prepare for visualization

1 Close your eyes. Take three deep breaths, breathing in calm and breathing out stress, anxieties and distracting thoughts.

2 The next seven breaths draw energy from the ground below you and the Earth below that, up through an imaginary column running through the center of your body.

3 The first breath lights up the energy point or *chakra* at the base of your spine, which is a red light or flower. The second lights the sacral chakra (below the belly button), which is orange. The third breath activates the solar plexus chakra which is yellow; the fourth the heart chakra which is green; the fifth the throat chakra which is blue; and the sixth the third-eye chakra (forehead) which is violet.

4 The seventh breath opens the crown chakra of pure white light. Allow it to shower over you and connect back with the Earth energy upon which you are drawing.

5 Visualize a circle of white light all around you. This creates sacred space between the everyday world and the inner world to which you are journeying.

6 When your visualization is over and you have made notes, close down the circle and the energy centers you have activated, leaving the base of spine chakra and crown chakra open just a little. Neglecting to close down can leave you over-sensitized and vulnerable to other people's negative energies.

7 Eat and drink something to ground yourself—this is important!

Meeting your patron deity

This exercise is suitable for those wishing to encounter a patron deity. Try not to preempt a choice of patron; let the right god or goddess choose you. You will be able to repeat this inner journey to visit your patron as much as you need to, to ask questions, receive knowledge, or spend time in their company. Aspects of this visualization are left open deliberately to allow your individual experience to fill in the gaps. Remember, the most significant details of your quest lie within you.

Details you encounter on your inner journeys are clues to guide you on your spiritual path.

VISUALIZATION

Undertake preparations as detailed on pages 138–139.

1 Close your eyes and enter the dark place behind your eyelids. Let your attention sink deeper and deeper into yourself, and when everything is dark and still, open your inner eyes to find yourself standing outside a stone gateway, behind which are sunlight, trees, birdsong and the scent of earth and flowers. Pass through to paths stretching into the distance both right and left. Choose one and set off down the path.

2 Notice the texture of the ground below your feet, the heat of the Sun and what you see all around you. You may see birds, animals, particular trees or plants. What sort of landscape do you find yourself in? Continue your journey, noting the detail of your surroundings.

3 The pathway forks into two or more paths. Choose one to explore and carry on walking. It will lead you into a particular terrain. Does it take you deep into a forest, a cave or uphill into open country? To water or into a building? You will reach your destination when you see an object lying on the path, on top of a hill, on an altar, or hanging from branches. Pick up the object—this is a gift from your patron and picking

it up signals your acceptance of their patronage. What is it? Does it have any particular significance which you need to remember in order to meditate on it later?

4 Become aware of a figure approaching you. This is your patron god or goddess. Note their appearance: The colors and the expression they wear; are they young or old; are they with any creatures or are they alone? Do they carry something that symbolizes their identity? Note any details that strike you as important.

5 Ask your patron any questions that seem pertinent to your spiritual development—about your chosen path, what advice they wish to offer or even their identity. Your deity may set you the task of finding this out for yourself. When you have finished talking, thank your deity for choosing you before retracing your steps back to the stone gateway.

6 Pass through the gateway back into darkness, then close your inner eyes. Slowly emerge to the place

behind your eyelids and, when ready, open your eyes and return to your surroundings.

7 Make notes of your journey before you forget the details and follow the instructions for 'closing down' on page 139.

Symbols that emerge during—and
following—your inner journey will guide
you toward your patron deity.

Over the next month you may
find features of your journey
turning up in everyday life as
coincidences or repetitions. You
may find your attention drawn to
particular symbols, images or
words. Try not to attach too
much meaning to such incidents,
nor to dismiss your recognition
of them as wishful thinking;
instead, write them down so that
you can form a judgement as patterns emerge.

When you find out the identity of your patron, do some research to find out
more about them. Consider why they have chosen you—what characteristic of
theirs relates to your personality or your life at the moment? What strength,
skills or knowledge do you think they can offer? Find a symbol or depiction of
your patron or create a symbol or representation of them to strengthen your
connection and to meditate upon.

Remember to make notes of everything
you see on your inner journey before you
forget the details.

Finding your spirit animal

This exercise is intended for those who wish to connect with their 'spirit' or totem animal. We have used animals as symbols of spiritual development and expressions of human identity for thousands of years; consequently, many pagans and witches draw upon animal symbolism in order to re-connect with our own animal nature. This visualization uses symbolism as a starting point, and it is up to you to honor your totem animal by committing yourself to take care of their relations on this planet.

Auroch (wild cow) in a 17,000-year-old cave painting, Lascaux, France.

VISUALIZATION

Undertake preparations as detailed on pages 138–139.

1 Close your eyes and allow your attention to sink into a dark place behind your eyelids. Imagine your body sinking into the ground, past the foundations of the building in which you are sitting, below the roots of trees and plants. Sink past the bones of the ancestors, the shells and remains of sea-creatures that swam in the prehistoric oceans. Imagine sinking into the white-hot metallic core of the planet. Sit in the Earth's centre, at the root and beginning of things.

2 When you are ready, imagine rising through all the layers to emerge between the roots of a great tree. Find yourself standing in lush, green surroundings. Notice the types of trees near by, whether it is day or night, sunny or moonlit, stormy or calm. Follow any path that attracts you, explore anything that catches your attention. Work your way toward a clearing

surrounded by ancient trees. Stand in the centre, arms spread wide, and mentally invite your appointed spirit animal to approach.

3 An ancient spirit of the wildwood will appear in the clearing. Note his appearance; do you recognize him? He will respond to your summons by swinging a giant club against the trunk of the largest tree three times before departing. (If he does not do this, it is a sign that you are not yet ready for this exercise. Follow the guidelines on page 139 for returning to your conscious state and try again no sooner than one lunar cycle following your first attempt.)

4 Wait patiently for your spirit animal to appear. Whatever it is, you must accept it as your totem beast and merge with it immediately. Take on the shape of the animal and allow it to take you wherever it roams. Trust the animal to take you where it will, and take careful note of what you do when you are shape-

changed, where you go and what is shown to you. The animal will let you know when it is time to depart. At this point, it will separate from you and you will regain human form. Note the animal, its appearance and characteristics. Remember to thank your spirit animal as it departs.

5 Close your inner eyes and sink once again into darkness. Do not retrace your journey; you have moved on and cannot return to where you were before you started. When you are ready, slowly return to a fully conscious state, to the room where you are sitting. Note down details of your journey and meeting with your totem animal and follow the instructions for closing down on page 139.

Imagine yourself in a clearing, surrounded by ancient trees.

In the days that follow this visualization you may be reminded of your animal spirit, mainly because your awareness is heightened by your encounter. Note any relevant coincidences that occur up to a Full-Moon cycle after your path-working, and do some research on your totem animal. What are its habits and characteristics in the wild? What does it symbolize that has relevance to your personality, your spiritual development or chosen path? As with the exercise for finding a patron deity, it is a good idea to acquire or make a suitable symbol or representation of your totem animal to focus on when meditating to further your connection with it.

Discovering your magical name

It is often a matter of great delight to new witches that we can choose "circle" or magical names for ourselves. This is the name we are known by within sacred space and which identify us to the deities and the elements, the guardians of the circle. A number of Wiccan traditions are associated with choosing a name (see exercises on pages 216–217), and you may like to combine them with this path-working. This visualization will guide you toward a first magical name, but don't be discouraged if it doesn't yield exact results the first time.

Opinion differs within the Wiccan community regarding how, when and to whom your magical name should be revealed. Some witches seem happy to take on their magical tag as an everyday name, though they may have a further, more closely kept name for circle purposes. Others have strict views about sharing a magical name, and keep this name for circle-space only. Whatever you, your coven or group protocols decide, you should never reveal another witch's magical name without permission. Names have power and should be treated with respect.

Pay attention to all images you encounter in your quest.

VIZUALIZATION

Undertake preparations as detailed on pages 138–139.

1 Close your eyes, relax and enter the space behind your eyelids. Go into the darkness within and feel yourself dropping through the levels of consciousness. Imagine yourself in an elevator descending many levels, until it stops and the doors open. Step out into a candlelit passage. Proceed along the passage, noting the texture of the floor on your bare feet, the material of the walls and any decorations that are present. Note whether the passage is straight or bent.

2 You come to a doorway leading to a chamber. Is the doorway covered by a curtain, a door or a screen, or is it open? Pass through into the room beyond, paying attention to details of your surroundings. At the center of the room is a tall plinth which you ascend by the means of steps. Approach whatever is on the plinth. The object holds a clue to your magical identity. Pick it up and inspect it, wear or eat it—whatever is appropriate to the object you find. When you are ready, step down from the plinth.

3 Notice a doorway leading out of the room—pass through this door into another passage. You may notice a flow of fresh air passing through the corridor as it leads you out into open terrain. What environment do you find yourself in? Is it day or night? What animals or plants, if any, surround you? Is there a preponderance of any one of the elements in this environment— lots of water or the presence of fire and heat? Spend some time here, as you may find further clues to your magical name. When ready, choose a spot to sit down and absorb the nature of this environment; wait for guidance to come.

4 You may be approached by a figure or an animal, or find your attention drawn to a tree, plant or some other aspect of this environment. This offers further clues to your magical name. You may even have this offered to you if a figure speaks with you. Whatever happens, remember to thank the figure, creature, tree, plant or element for their guidance.

5 When the surroundings have yielded all that they are prepared to in respect of your magical name, close your inward eyes and move back into the darkness. Mentally step into your "elevator" and feel yourself ascending to the level of everyday consciousness. Slowly return to your surroundings, open your eyes ready to note the significant aspects of your inner journey. Follow the instructions on page 139 for closing down.

Finding a magical name may take time and patience. You can combine this exercise with guidance offered on pages 216–217, or continue to meditate on it and take careful note of aspects that appear in your everyday life. Often such coincidences are the result of your enhanced attention and should be noted.

Clues to your magical name may be found around you in everyday life.

The temple of the Moon

In the mystical Qabalah (see pages 302–307), the sphere of the Moon is called "Yesod" and is associated with the unconscious mind, with cycles of existence and with psychic and magical abilities. This ties in with the symbolism and experiences that witches associate with the Moon, and is a good starting point for those who wish to discover more about their spiritual direction. The following is a favorite in more traditional covens where newcomers are trained by a high priest or priestess.

This inner journey helps new Wiccans move beyond the realm of the rational and into what I call "Goddess-space." This is the chaotic place-time of possibility and potential, the foundation of all creation and magic, which those who seek a magical life must experience. We need to be in touch with Moon energy to grow spiritually and extend our powers magically. This is a potent visualization, so it is advisable to leave at least three lunar cycle between visits.

The Moon is the ruler of dreams.

VIZUALIZATION

Undertake preparations as detailed on pages 138–139.

1 Close your eyes and concentrate on breathing in through your nose and out through your mouth, thinking only of your breathing. When fully relaxed, allow your attention to sink deep into yourself, dropping from the head to the throat chakra, then to the heart and further down to your solar plexus. Allow your attention to sink further until you come to rest at your center.

2 Imagine yourself on a dark beach with only the light of the stars to pick out the details of your surroundings. Walk toward the waves breaking on the sand and into the water. How does the water feel? Is it cold and refreshing or warm and embracing?

3 Walk into the deep water until the waves cover your head and you are walking on the seabed. You can breathe and move quite easily in this environment. Walk until the seabed ascends and you emerge from the waves on another shore. Walk forwards onto the beach. The Moon has risen; note its phase. Walk along the shore until you come to a path through the greenery that surrounds the beach. What kind of trees and plants are found here?

4 Follow the path leading toward a white marble building. Note its shape. Move toward the door, taking note of its features, and open it. Enter the building; the door will close behind you. Move to the center of the space, where moonlight pours down. Is the building roofed or open to the elements? In the surrounding walls are many curtains, hiding doorways. Choose one to go through. Draw its curtain aside, noting the color and any symbols, and push open the door. This may lead into an open space or another building. Pass through the door into the realm you have chosen.

5 A figure either waits for you or will approach you. Allow them to speak first—they have a gift from the temple of the Moon for you. Accept it with thanks. Spend some time inspecting the object. Hold it to your chest and allow it to merge into your spirit-body through your solar plexus. Allow its essence to ascend, with your attention, from solar plexus to heart, from heart to throat, and from throat to your third-eye chakra.

6 When ready, slowly return to everyday consciousness and make notes of all that has passed during your journey. Close down in accordance with the guidance on pages 139.

The Moon card in the Tarot represents psychic abilities.

The object you have been given may appear in your dreams, which should be more vivid following this path-working. Meditate on the Moon card in the Tarot— what does the Moon teach those who are on the Wiccan path? Spend time connecting with the lunar cycle, noting its impact on your dreams and psychic abilities, noting changes in your energy levels throughout the month. Most importantly, see if you can discover what your gift represents in terms of your magical skills.

elemental balancing

Given that one of the key concerns of Wicca is to restore balance to our lives and our relationship with the Earth, it is not surprising that we focus on finding that balance within ourselves. One way we do this is through our relationship with the elements Air, Fire, Water and Earth. We may find ourselves working more with one element than with others; for example, when I am writing, I feel most connected with Air. This is a natural reflection of our work with the sacred elements. However, we may find ourselves over-dependent on one element, or have problems relating to a particular element for no apparent reason. The best way to address this is to balance the elements within us.

This visualization is suited to all seekers of balance. You can use it as many times as you wish, and most covens have a version that they use as a way of grounding before magical work or as a part of training.

You can see the elements at work in nature in the sun, wind and rain.

VIZUALIZATION

Prior to undertaking the preparations as detailed on pages 138–139, give yourself a good physical shakedown to loosen joints and muscles, and brush away your everyday anxieties and concerns.

1 When your breathing has slowed, lie on the ground and make yourself comfortable. Close your eyes and allow your attention to sink deep into your body.

2 Imagine yourself sinking through your body, through the floor and down into the Earth below. Sink deeply into the layers of clay, chalk, rock and hollows beneath. Move deeper still, feeling the weight of all the layers of roots, plants, seeds, fungi, loam, stones and bones above you. Sink further still, until you lie within a cavern. What do you see there? What do you smell? What do you feel? Allow your own body to merge with the matter around you, until there is no distinction between

your body and the Earth-body. Stay in this state as long as you are able.

3 When you are ready, notice the moisture around you. Warm water washes the edges of your body so that you become aware of a separation between yourself and the Earth. The flow increases until you are entirely surrounded, floating in a sac of clear water. You can breathe easily as you float within it. Become aware of the flow around you and within you. Feel the blood coursing through your veins, the water of your body tissue. Allow yourself to merge with the water and let it carry you out of your Earth-womb into a sea, pulsing with currents and flows of different temperature.

4 Become one with the current and flow and the waves that break on the shore. Spend as much time as you are able merged with Water.

5 When ready, allow the current to

wash you ashore on to a warm beach, where the Sun dries your skin. Take a draught of Air into your lungs and exhale fully. Take in three deep breaths and exhale as far as you can. On the next breath, feel yourself rise above the sand and on the next, rise higher, suspended above the beach. Allow each breath to take you higher, and let your body float on the currents of Air. Imagine the breezes blowing your spirit-body along. Experiment with flight and swoop through the sky. Become aware of the oxygen pulsing through your blood, giving essential energy to your body. Rise higher and stay in flight for as long as you wish.

6 When ready, rise toward the heat and light of the Sun. Allow yourself to absorb its energy and become aware of the heat of your own body. Rise until you are absorbed into the Sun's fire, becoming completely radiant and filled with light and warmth. Merge your spirit-body with the body of the Sun, lighting the solar system with your strength. How does this feel? Remain in this state for as long as you wish or are able.

7 When ready, slowly return to your surroundings, bringing with you the energy and gifts of the elements with which you have merged. Carry that awareness with you throughout your rituals and spell-work, or when you wish to restore balance in your life. Close down according to the guidance on page 139.

Samhain journey

This is the first of a set of seasonal visualizations intended to help you celebrate specific festivals. You can undertake these journeys individually or nominate a member of your group to lead you through these path-workings. You will notice that Yule and Ostara are missing; these have been appropriated to some extent by Christianity and by secular society. The challenge is to construct your own inner journeys for these festivals, in order to help you encounter an authentic Yule and Eostre. Read through and experience some of the visualizations offered here for ideas.

Samhain is the day of the ancestors, the time to honor our dead. We may speak with them, but we may not join them on the Isle of the Dead. There aren't many "don'ts" in this book but please observe this warning—if you try to cross over, you may find your dreams disturbed, or your psychic development hampered quite seriously.

The Samhain journey takes us to the Isle of the Dead.

VISUALIZATION

Before undertaking preparations as detailed on pages 138–139, ensure that you are properly grounded, and have a familiar object close at hand that you can physically hold when you return from your inner journey. This will help to anchor you in consensual reality when the visualization has ended.

1 Close your eyes and become aware of any intrusive thoughts. Mentally bat them away as you prepare to enter the inner worlds.

2 As you enter the space within, become aware of the wash of waves in the distance. Allow this sound to become louder as you draw nearer to its source. Open your inner senses— feel the drag of breezes on your skin, the taste of salt, the sensation of dry sand under your feet. Open your inner vision to see that you are on a seashore. Take note of your surroundings. What color is the sand, the sky? Walk to the water's edge until you find a craft. Step into

the boat and notice its color, its details. Is anybody else in the boat? Do they speak to you? What do you notice as the boat moves out to sea? What do you hear?

3 When the boat lands, notice the details of its mooring place. This is a small island, joined to a vaster shore by a bridge. What does the bridge look like; what and who is on the other shore? You may hear voices or sounds that are familiar and strange, see faces you know and faces of strangers. Those who wish to speak to you will approach the far end of the bridge. You may face them from your side of the bridge, but you may not cross. If anybody wishes to speak with you, they will do so. You may speak with the dead; you are contacting that deep part of yourself that is their memory. When you have finished speaking, bid farewell and thank the guardian of the bridge for your time there. You may ask the guardian who they are and what their purpose is. Listen

carefully to the answers; you may wish to remember and note them down on your return.

4 Rest on your island. Think about your own life. What is your earliest memory? What have you learned during your lifetime so far? Who taught you these lessons? Are they alive or have they passed to the Summerlands? What part of them remains with you? When ready, return to the boat, and sail back to the shore from whence you came. How do you feel to leave that place? Is the journey back more difficult than the journey outward? Who is with you on your journey?

5 As you disembark, thank whoever travels with you and concentrate on the feeling of firm ground beneath your feet. Physically pick up the object you have chosen as your anchor and slowly return to your surroundings. If you are working with others, you may wish to compare your experiences before you make notes and close down (as indicated on page 139).

Eat a hearty meal after this particular journey—stamping your feet on *terra firma* is also a good antidote to any residual dreaminess! Over the next month, revisit the notes you made following your visualization and see what lessons you can take from your journey to the farthest shore.

Ensure that you anchor yourself on your return from the Samhain journey.

Imbolc reawakening

Imbolc witnesses the first signs of returning life after the darker days of the year. It is a time to sow seeds for new projects and renew our commitment to the principles we hold dear. This visualization helps emerge from the deep womb of winter, the darker days when our spiritual attention is turned inward, into the light of the coming season when our attention will be turned outward. Then we will work toward manifesting the ideas and potential we have discovered in the dark within ourselves.

This path-working acts as a catalyst to effect changes from within; at Imbolc we begin to move from concept or potential, to manifestation. Parts of this guided journey will require physical movement, so you will need to ensure adequate floor space, and some pillows or cushions to support your changing resting positions.

Imbolc is a time of emergence.

VISUALIZATION

Undertake the preparations detailed on pages 138–139.

1 On the floor, take up your normal sleeping position. When settled, close your eyes and concentrate on your heartbeat for 30 beats. Tune into this pulse as it slows, and if you cannot hear it, imagine the sound. Through the floor, try to feel another great, slow heartbeat. It matches yours. Follow that heartbeat down, deep into the spaces below the floor, through the supports and foundations of the building down into the Earth, roots, clay and chalk of the rich soil.

2 As your attention sinks deeper, hear the heartbeat below you growing louder—you may even feel it. Let your heartbeat slow to match the heartbeat of the Earth body. When these heartbeats match, allow your heartbeat to merge with that of the Earth. Concentrate on this shared heartbeat. What do you feel? Are you aware of other life within you? Do you feel sleepy or awake and alive?

3 Become aware of the seeds, bulbs, tubers and roots within the Earth body. What does the Earth offer them? What do they take from the

Earth? Move your attention toward a seed. Merge with that seed and become the life within it. Physically imitate how you feel as the life within that seed. Staying in that position, think about the potential and the ideas that lie within you. How are these like and/or unlike the life in the seed? Allow this potential, these ideas, to merge with you-as-seed.

4 Consider this carefully, then become aware of the soil around you warming up. Become aware of nourishing warmth coming down from the surface. What does this do to the life within you? Physically imitate how you think the life within the seed responds to the heat. Become aware of the light of the surface coming closer to you. Physically mimic the effect this has on the life within you, the seed. Continue the process of the seed's response to the sunlight. Continue moving in response to how you feel as seed/potential within. When the process is complete, open your eyes. What physical position are you in? If you can, keep this position and

slowly return your consciousness to human form. When you have completed this change, close your eyes again and assume a comfortable standing or sitting position, whichever is closest to the position in which you find yourself.

5 What potential or ideas did you identify within yourself? Are you aware of how these came into being? What protects/shelters and nourishes these? What spurs them toward growth? What will continue to feed them when they have grown and flourished? What would prevent them from growing to maturity and producing other "seeds"? How will you ensure that they come to manifestation and fruition?

6 When you are satisfied that you have answered these questions, relax and listen to your heartbeat still merged with the Earth. Listen and feel for 30 heartbeats, then separate yours and slowly shift your consciousness toward your physical surroundings before returning to consensual reality.

7 If you carry out this exercise in a group, you may wish to compare your experiences before you note down the most significant aspects of your journey. Return to these ideas over the following spring and summer months to check that you have tended the seeds of your ideas, and that your new ideas and projects are not left behind. Close down in accordance with the guidelines on page 139.

Just as mighty trees grow from the smallest seeds, amazing things can materialize from the seeds of your ideas.

Beltane and the Green Man

The beginning of May (end of October in the southern hemisphere) heralds the first blossom of the hawthorn tree. The greenwoods and meadows flourish and the Green Man, consort of the Goddess, puts aside the wilder part of his nature to marry her under the oak. To enter the realm of the Green Man is to encounter the wilder side of our own natures and to fully appreciate our physicality. This visualization is best undertaken outdoors, and works well for solo path-workers as well as with a group. If you are working alone you could take along a friend to guarantee your privacy and safety. Take along a little bread and fruit juice.

VISUALIZATION

Prior to undertaking the preparations detailed on pages 138–139, find a leafy tree with a large trunk against which you can sit and lean your back while you are journeying.

1 Close your eyes and concentrate on the touch of the tree bark against your back. Allow yourself to feel the warmth and life in the tree. Listen to any sounds coming from within it, from its branches. Focus your attention on the tree, and imagine your body taking on some of its characteristics. Which characteristics would you wish to take on, symbolically, emotionally or physically? Which would you prefer not to acquire? Why?

The greenwood has an important place in the pagan imagination.

2 When you have answered these questions and mentally taken on those aspects of the tree that you wish to, become aware of the most desirable aspects of your own physical body. Try to identify something you like about your physical self. Now imagine that you hear someone approach. Open your inner eyes and greet the figure who stands before you. Do you recognize the figure or any aspect of him or her? Is the figure alone or accompanied? What is he or she carrying? The figure lays an object on the ground before you or offers it to you to take. They are honoring the aspects of your physical self that you have identified as attractive or especially likeable. Accept this gift— take note of what it is as this may be important to you in future.

3 The figure invites you to follow them—allow your spirit-body to do this. How does the figure move? Do you adjust your movement to match theirs? Who or what else accompanies you? Allow the figure

to lead you deep into the greenwood, taking note of all the life teeming around you. Be aware of the sensation of the forest floor on your feet, the brush of the Sun and breeze on your body, and the scents that rise from the ground. If you see anything edible, taste it. What can you hear?

What activities are taking place around you? Do you feel able to join in? Why?

Use what you find around you to decorate yourself—blossoms, feathers or trailing leaves. Be conscious of how your physical body is responding to the activities of your spirit-self.

4 Deep in the forest, you see a very old building. Go toward it and explore. What is its condition? What symbols do you find among its decorations or structure? Do they tell you anything about the realm in which you are journeying or the figure(s) you encounter there? What do they tell you about your chosen spiritual path/yourself? When you are ready to leave, approach the figure that has led you there, and thank them for your experience. They may speak with you—listen to what they have to say and accept anything they have to offer you.

5 Allow the scene around you to fade. Direct your attention to the tree trunk against your back. Slowly separate from the tree, mentally allowing the physical aspects you acquired during your journey to fade. Keep within you any symbolic and emotional aspects you adopted from it; this is a gift from the greenwood. Gently return to everyday consciousness and to your surroundings. After you have jotted down any notes, close down in accordance with the guidelines on page 139.

6 Finally eat the bread and drink some fruit juice, leaving a little to pour into the Earth to honor the tree which has been your guardian; leave some bread for the birds.

The stag is a symbol of Herne, guardian of the greenwood.

Litha and the turning of the wheel

The summer solstice is the longest day of the year and many witches take to the hillsides and sacred places to greet the Litha sunrise. The visualization for this festival is intended for those staying out to witness the turning of the year's wheel. Ideally, it is a journey to be undertaken just before the sky grows light. If you are working alone, ensure that you will be secure and private. You will need a blanket or mat to sit on and a chalice or wineglass of orange juice.

VISUALIZATION

Prior to undertaking the preparations detailed on pages 138–139, find a comfortable place to sit at a vantage point facing east, so that you can view the sunrise. Place the chalice of juice on the ground in front of you.

1 Close your eyes and concentrate on the space behind your eyelids. Sink into the darkness within and let your attention sink from the level of your third-eye chakra to your throat, to your heart chakra and on down until it rests at your solar plexus. Focus on this energy point in your body. Picture it as a fiery wheel, growing in brilliance until it radiates outward from your body, lighting everything around you. Allow it to diminish slightly, retaining the image of the golden spinning wheel within.

2 Consider the function of this energy point in your body. How does this part of your body react in stressful situations, surprises or shocks? How would it feel to have this energy point in an open position all of the time?

3 Relax and become aware of the ground where you sit, the life on and beneath its surface. Sensitize yourself to the temperature of the air so that you can become aware of any changes as dawn breaks. Keeping an awareness of your solar plexus energy point, allow your attention to drop further down into the deep core of the Earth. Carry your awareness though the levels of life and death that form the layers to the center. Drop down toward the heat and light of the Earth's core. Envisage its gases and flames emerging as sulfur, steam, geysers, lava and volcanoes. Imagine the metallic core of the planet as an inner sun, shooting flames, gases and minerals into the Earth-space

The turning of the year is seen as a wheel or circle in Wicca.

around it, enriching the soil and providing energy and fuel to the upper world.

4 Now transfer that thought to your own solar plexus; picture it still as a fiery wheel, spinning at the center of your torso. What energy does this Sun-wheel provide for your body/emotions/spirit? How does it direct or distribute energy in/from your body? Experience this by drawing energy up from the Earth's core into your own solar plexus, and direct it through your solar plexus toward the circle of light with which you have surrounded yourself, allowing the energy to circle around you. What does this power feel like? Allow the energy circulating around you to be drawn back through the spinning wheel of your solar plexus and return to the Earth core below.

5 As you sense it growing lighter and the temperature rising, draw into your solar plexus the heat and light from the Sun, which, though below the horizon, is already making its presence felt. Now direct the energy you are drawing from the Earth through your spinning solar plexus to the sky, and from sky via solar plexus, to Earth. Absorb into yourself some of the light and energy you are transferring between Earth and sky.

6 Continue until the Sun rises. Stand to greet the Sun, cupping in your hands the chalice of juice. Allow the Sun's rays to fall on the liquid, and when the Sun is fully risen, drink the liquid. The energy that you take into yourself now will carry you through the darker days to come. When you write up your notes, consider the image of the wheel in relation to the dance between Earth and Sun, Sun and self. Close down according to the guidance offered on page 139.

Stonehenge in Wiltshire, England, is aligned with the summer solstice sunrise.

Lughnasadh—winnowing and gathering

At harvest time our thoughts turn toward the gifts and blessings we have accumulated in the past year. This is a good time to evaluate our own personal "harvests" and consider which of these we can share with others. It is also a time for sorting out the wheat from the chaff—both literally and metaphorically speaking. Just as the stalks and hulls are separated from the nourishing grain, we can decide what things to discard, and which to keep and value.

Ripened corn represents both seed and harvest.

VISUALIZATION

This visualization can take place indoors or out, in a group or alone. You need a pen and paper, a short length of pure wool thread and a few stalks of corn, preferably from this year's harvest. If working outdoors, it would be ideal to have a small bonfire close by. Undertake the preparations detailed on pages 138–139.

1 Holding the corn, close your eyes and focus on the life cycle it represents—from seed to green shoot, then tall stalk with ears of corn turning from green to gold beneath the Sun, producing more seed, and so on.

2 Now think of your life since the last harvest. How have you progressed and grown? What aspects of self, projects or ideas have flourished? Have you harvested these or are they still in the process of growth? What bounty and blessings have come to you in the past year? Think in terms of wealth (having enough food, shelter, warmth), health, opportunities, things you have been able to create, things that have been given freely to you, emotional support from friends, new people who have come into your life. How would you summarize these blessings? Try to encapsulate these blessings in one word. Keep that word in your head for later.

3 Now think about things that have stayed too long in your life, are no longer needed or are simply unwelcome. These can be habits, the presence of certain conditions or people, burdens, physical objects, things you have outgrown. How would you characterize these unwanted things? Try once again to capture this chaff in a single word. Remember it for later.

Harvest is a time to consider our blessings, and what we can carry forward into the next cycle.

4 Consider what you would like to carry from this harvest into next year. Imagine these blessings as stalks of corn, tied in a sheaf, arranged in stacks and placed in a

basket before you. Who would you like to share your bounty with? How might you do that? How does it feel to have the fruits of your labor and gifts laid in front of you in this way? Think forward to next harvest—what would you like to see in that basket? What do you want to achieve in the next year? Who can help you do that and how will you ensure that you have the opportunity to accomplish all that you wish in the next turn of the wheel?

5 Become aware of a figure sitting opposite you. What do they look like? Do they carry anything with them? Do they ask you for anything? Do they give you anything? Offer this year's harvest to them and await their response. Do they accept? What message do they have for you? Thank them for any gifts or advice they have to offer and then allow them to rise, walk away and/or fade into the distance.

6 Gently return to everyday consciousness, open your eyes and, on the right-hand side of the paper, write the word that encapsulates your blessings. On the left-hand side write the word that describes those things you wish to discard. Tear the paper down the middle, and with the wool attach the blessing word to your small bunch of corn. Scrunch the other word up into a ball and either throw it into the fire, or burn it outside afterward. If you are able to retrieve its ash, mix this with some compost or bury near a plant so that it can be recycled as nourishment. If you are working with a group, you may wish to exchange corn blessings or keep your own. Either way, the blessings should be kept until Imbolc, then burned outside and the ashes used as compost. Ensure that you close down after this path-working in accordance with the advice offered on page 139.

Modron—Arthur's journey

In the wheel of the year, the autumn equinox is positioned in the west. Our pagan ancestors believed that this was the direction of death, the route taken by the soul on its way to the Summerlands. Day and night are in perfect balance at Modron, and thereafter dark triumphs and we say a sad farewell to the Sun as it "goes into the west." The legend of King Arthur has particular resonance at this time of year; he is the archetypal Sun King, the consort of the Earth Goddess, borne away into the west when his time is spent.

Our ancestors believed that souls migrated to the Summerlands, in the west where the sun sets.

VISUALIZATION

This visualization can be used as part of a Modron ritual or as preparation for it. It is suitable for a group or individuals. If you are able to do this outdoors, a waterside location is ideal. You will need to stand and move around at the beginning of this meditation so ensure that you have ample space. Have a blue candle in a holder close to hand. Undertake the preparations outlined on pages 138–139.

1 Stand with eyes open facing north, the place where the Sun sits below the horizon. How do you feel when you face this direction? With what do you associate it? Turn toward the east, the place of the sunrise and dawn. How do you feel when you face this direction? With what do you associate it?

2 Turn on your heel to your right again, facing south, where the Sun is at its zenith at noon. How do you feel when you face this direction? With what do you associate it? Continue your turn and face full west. This is the direction of the sunset, of dusk. Sit down, still facing west, and close your eyes.

3 With your mind's eye, picture a seascape, the sea gently rocking. The Sun is sinking toward the horizon, glowing orange in the sky and throwing its reflected rays across the water, lighting a path toward the sunset. How does this scene make you feel?

4 There is a craft setting sail toward the Sun. What color are its sails? What is in the boat? Think back to the days of summer just passed. What did that summer bring you? What did it take away? Do you have any regrets of things done or left undone; relationships that ended? On the shore is a quiver of arrows and a bow next to a small fire. Each arrow represents the things that summer has brought and taken away again. Mentally name each arrow with something the summer brought as you pick them up and fix them to the bow. Dip each tip into the fire. Take aim and shoot the flaming arrows over the water into the sails and hull of the departing boat. Continue until you have fired all arrows. Raise your right hand in farewell to the boat and everything that you have sent with it; watch it sail away until you can no longer see it. When it has disappeared, the rim of the Sun will sink below the horizon.

5 Allow this vision to fade and gradually return to your surroundings. Before you make any notes or close down, consider all the gifts of summer, both personal and communal. Think about the Sun's warmth and how it warmed and ripened the crops and fruits. Remember how it enabled people to get together outdoors, to carry out pursuits closed to them in winter. Think about good times you shared with friends and/or family during the warm season. Give thanks to the Sun and light your blue candle in memory of summer's happy days. When you make notes, ask yourself what you associate with the west and how the Sun's demise affects you emotionally, physically or spiritually. Close down in accordance with the guidance offered on page 139.

the
sacred
circle

The circle

I am a circle within a circle
With no beginning and never ending.

(POPULAR PAGAN CHANT)

The circle represents a universal and spiritually relevant paradox—a shape without beginning and without end. It visually describes eternity, the mysterious cycles of existence and the often uncanny circularity of our own lives.

Our ancient ancestors recognized the sacred significance of this shape and laid out many of their monuments in circle form. Around Europe, for example, are the scattered remains of wooden and stone circles, aligned with specific stellar or solar rises and settings, many of which contain inner circles.

Many commentators have noted the yonic symbolism attached to such formations—that the circle represents that sacred place in the body from which women push life into the world. The fact that there are circles within circles seems to confirm the mystical association between the physical act of giving birth and the mystery of regeneration.

In Wicca, we do most of our ritual and spell-work within a circle, cast by a witch in order to define the boundaries of

The circle symbolizes the miraculous cycle of existence.

the place where we come face to face with our deities, where we work magic and enter altered states of consciousness. This space is sacred because it is dedicated to the God and Goddess and their work. It also contains what we call the "space between the worlds," a place that is neither wholly set in the everyday nor wholly in the realm of Spirit, but marked out and set aside for the wise who can travel between these worlds and bring back wisdom. The space is dedicated to the god or goddess within us, as well as the God and Goddess of the rest of the existence.

Every time we step into the circle, we are honoring the divine within ourselves and growing and developing our sacred potential in the company of the deity.

SACRED SPACE

The boundaries of the circle are protected by the elements and the deities we call in and honor. This is not to protect us from B-movie type monsters or demons that we may inadvertently raise or attract through our work—it doesn't work like that! The circle protects us from the crowding distraction of everyday concerns, so that we can stand back from the minutiae of our busy lives. It allows us to temporarily set aside the mantle of our daily roles. The boundaries we set allow us to claim the space as specific to a sacred purpose, as special.

The line of the circle is a boundary—it allows us to contain the power we raise within it and holds it until we are ready to release it into the wider world to do its work. In this respect, it is a little like a pot with a lid, in which we are boiling a good soup—we wouldn't place the ingredients on the plate before they were properly cooked, so we keep the lid on the pan until it is ready. It is exactly the same with magic and ritual work—the ingredients of the spell or ritual need to be properly energized and blended before they are ready to emerge as a power and energy in the wider web of existence.

SPACE BETWEEN WORLDS

An important point to note is that the sacred circle is not a flat, two-dimensional shape; it is actually a sphere that encompasses the whole sacred space. It extends above and below the human participants, intersecting floors and ceilings and often walls. It is a world both within and outside of the world of our everyday existence or consensual reality; it allows us to step outside of that reality and into another—while at the same time remaining connected with our baseline everyday existence. Circle-space is also a part of the world of Spirit, the place of connection, interconnection, formation and transformation. This is another paradox of the circle; it offers a space between the worlds, but incorporates aspects of those worlds at the same times as it provides a space apart from them.

Ancient spiral carvings on stone, Newgrange Mound, Ireland.

Just as the spherical nature of the sacred space provides us with a perfected and whole circle, a reflection of itself above and below the line of the ground on which we physically work, so the worlds between which we work are reflected within that space. As we say in Wicca: "As above: So below." The nature of the circle makes it possible for us to symbolize, represent and encapsulate aspects of our daily world, and enact symbolic changes that we wish to actualize within consensual reality. We use the symbolic as a doorway through which we can touch and then draw through threads from the world of Spirit, which we then weave into a new pattern. This is how magic works—by accessing the worlds between which we move and bringing them together. Ironically, in order to do so, we first have to move outside of both; and this means going into the sacred space of the circle.

EVER-CHANGING

Another shape closely associated with the circle is the spiral—a progressive circle that if seen three-dimensionally might closely resemble an elongated spring. Some Wiccans acknowledge the close links between the spiral and the circle because we see the circle as a symbol of constant change and progression. Nothing in the Universe stays the same and this is true of the circle. For us, just as all gods and goddesses are one God and Goddess but not all gods and goddesses are

the same, all circles are the one great circle of being, but every circle is different. We do not ever come out of the circle exactly the same person who goes in; it is like the saying that one can never cross the same river twice. By definition, the river changes because time passes, and the same is true of the circle. Within this progression of changes, the circle can be seen as a simple expression of the spiral—symbol of the eternal flux of all time-space-matter.

MAGNIFYING OUR EXPERIENCE

There is an additional and important reason why each circle is different; it is the space of transformation. If the circle is different each time, it is also true that whatever we take with us becomes altered in some way as a result of stepping

into it. Some witches notice early on that there is a sort of magnifying effect at work within sacred space; this is a natural consequence of the intensity of what we experience there, and ensues from close contact with the realm of Spirit. What we carry with us to the circle grows in our consciousness to the point where we can see it

The spiral expresses the eternal journey of time-space-matter.

properly, occasionally becoming so big that we have to deal with it. This can be anything from a strength that we are failing to recognize and develop, to a bad habit that needs to be dealt with.

What we deal out to others within the circle, as in life, is what is returned to us; it is what we become. In the circle, this effect is amplified manifold.

TIME LAPSE

You may notice when you begin circle-work that there is a slight discrepancy in time perception between the world of consensual reality and the space between the worlds. Many witches notice that occasionally what seems to be no more than an hour in the circle is three hours or more outside of it. The most common experience seems to be the rapidity with which time passes in circle-space. It is not unknown, however, for the reverse to be experienced, especially when deep meditation work is being undertaken. On such occasions, celebrants may leave the circle feeling as though they have been away for hours, and find that only 45 minutes has passed. In tales of the Celtic Otherworld, human visitors to the world of Faery invariably experience a sense of time-disorientation; what passes for a day in the realm of Faery is found to be a year in the mortal realm, and seven years becomes seven hundred. It is tempting to speculate on the origins of these peculiar time-lapses, and whether the tales have absorbed aspects of tribal shamanic practice, where those who walk between the worlds experience time-changes.

The shape of the circle also describes the progression of our planet around the Sun. The circle is always cast *deosil* (pronounced day-sill) or "sunwise"—clockwise. Traditionally, when building magical and ritual energy, celebrants try to ensure that they move deosil while in the circle to keep the energy moving in the right direction. Sometimes participants will move *widdershins* or anti-sunwise—anti-clockwise, when a banishing ritual is being enacted. When you become familiar with the energies that you work with as a witch, you will be able to decide what works best once you are within sacred space. However, the circle is almost universally cast deosil in Wicca.

Our ancestors left clues to their spiritual beliefs on the landscape.

Altars and sacred spaces

The classic definition of an altar is a place upon which sacrifices or gifts are offered to deities; if a physical description accompanies this definition, it suggests that an altar is a "raised" structure or a "high place." Although this is a narrow idea of what an altar is, it does convey the notion that it holds things that are sacred and special, and may be a space in which gifts or offerings are left. In Wicca, our deities do not demand sacrifice; this much is clear in the Mother Charge—the words of the Goddess to the people, usually spoken in the circle by one of the participants (see pages 232–233). However, we do use altars in Wicca for several functions.

Altars come in many shapes and forms. They can be as simple as a flat rock placed in a shaded corner of a garden or woodland or as elaborate as an indoor permanent table decorated with embroidered cloths, canopied and covered in candles, statues or other sacred imagery. They might be temporary—for example, an altar set up for the duration of a circle and then dismantled. An altar can be a corner shelf in an apartment or a marble table on a hillside, but what really matters is the intent with which it is used. Its sacred purpose is what makes it an altar.

Incense is often used to consecrate sacred space.

SACRED CIRCLE ALTARS

An altar provides a focal point for sacred and magical activity within the circle. Traditionally set up in the north, but sometimes placed at the center, the place of Spirit, the altar holds the tools and ingredients of ritual and may hold wands, *athames* (witches' knives), chalices, pentacles, initiation cords (see pages 200–201 and 226–229), bowls of salt and water, herbs, candles, crystals, mortar and pestle, or depictions of the

Altars provide a focus for spell-work and spiritual development.

deities. It also provides a practical working surface upon which to mix herbs, anoint candles, "exorcise" water and bless salt (see pages 198–199). The ingredients for spells, once carried out, sometimes rest here until the end of the circle. When tools, spells or items need blessing or consecrating for a sacred purpose, they are brought to the altar—a place where things are made sacred, not just a place where sacred things are housed.

OUTSIDE ALTARS

Outside of the circle, altars serve many different purposes. In my garden, the big flat stone surrounded by many other rounder stones, planted around with rock roses and rosemary, is an altar to the Goddess. I have to sit on the ground to work on it, which brings me physically down to Earth. I use it as a focal point when I want to talk to the Goddess or a particular goddess, and I can burn

Altars can be placed indoors or outside.

incense and leave flowers or stones on it as offerings to her. In my home, the mantelpiece above the main hearth is an altar which variously houses offerings to particular goddesses, the physical ingredients for ongoing spell-work, candles and little offerings—feathers, flowers, cards, which honor the Goddess within. I have friends who have built altars that resemble shrines, out of stones and rocks and woven copper wire—these are focal points for meditation and visual journeys, spell-work, gifts to the Goddess, and a place to light candles to remember the dead.

In the open there are often natural altars, especially at ancient sites; these may be rocks where people leave coins, feathers, herbs or seeds for the birds and animals that frequent the place, or even a space on the ground below an old tree, or before a sacred well or spring. Sometimes trees near such places are dressed with "clouties"—ribbons or strips of material that contain wishes or are simply devotional offerings to the deities of that place. If you do build an altar or leave devotional offerings at an outdoor space, it is particularly important that you use biodegradable materials so that, in time, they return to nature without polluting the environment.

Building an altar in your home is relatively simple—decide its purpose, find a suitable location and gather to it those items that you feel will best serve its function. Choose appropriate symbols, colors and items for it through meditation, intuition and research (see pages 78–89 and 210–211). Once you have built your own altar, whether it is a corner shelf with a tealight and a few shells and stones, or an elaborate shrine hung with embroidered cloths, treat it with the respect that it, you and the God and Goddess deserve.

Salt and water are used to cleanse indoor space in preparation for ritual.

Circle-work

The space in which a circle is cast is customarily cleared of both physical and psychic detritus. If indoors, the space is traditionally cleansed by scattering specially prepared salt water all around it.

The water is first exorcised; this requires you to relax, draw in energy from the Earth through your energy points (chakras) and direct it through your hand to the water to drive out all surplus energies it may have absorbed. The form of words can range from the traditional: "I exorcise thee O creature of water that

thou cast out from thee all uncleanlinesses and impurities"; to the more basic: "I cleanse you in the name of the Goddess." The same hand is used to bless the salt, a natural purifier, saying: "Blessings upon this creature of salt, may all malignancy be cast hence from that all good enter herein"; or "The blessings of the Goddess be upon this salt." It is then poured into the water, stirred together either with a few words: "May this salt water serve to purify this space and bless my art"; or with no words at all.

Circle-work with others can be empowering and inspiring.

The salt water is scattered around the room deosil, starting in the east, then sprinkled over the participants. It is then time to cast the circle (see pages 202–203). In the open, however, salt and water should not be used as this will kill plant life where it is scattered, and open space in a natural setting does not need cleansing or purifying in the same way as indoor space which is also used for other purposes.

SETTING THE ELEMENTS

Prior to cleansing the space, you should set up the quarters— the directions for the sacred elements. Candles, cloths and symbols for Air, Fire, Water and Earth are placed around the circle in the cardinal directions east, south, west and north respectively. Corresponding colors for each are: yellow for Air, red for Fire, blue for Water, and green for Earth. In the center, a purple or white candle represents Spirit. If you find it difficult to obtain colored candles, tealights work just as well. Some circles decorate the quarters with symbols relevant to the appropriate element—a feather for Air, a lamp for Fire, a shell for Water and a pebble for Earth.

There are magical tools associated with circle-work. Some witches like to use an athame to do the salt and water blessing and to cast the circle. This is a special knife, usually black-handled, that has been consecrated for use in circle-work. It is usually blessed by dipping the blade in Water, showing it to Fire, plunging it through Air and into Earth before being consecrated in the circle. This knife is generally used only by its owner—though some witches allow others to use it in circle-work. Finding, making or preparing an athame is often a task given to a witch in preparation for initiation (see pages 226–229). Depending on the tradition in which you work, it is associated with either Fire or Air.

THE CHALICE AND PENTACLE

The chalice is associated with Water and is traditionally given to a witch, as it represents the element of love. This contains the wine or juice that is passed around the circle before the end of a ritual and can be used in spell-work (see pages 252–265). The wine is blessed, sipped, then passed deosil, with a kiss, with the words: "May you never thirst" or "Blessed Be." Some witches use a pentacle—a five-pointed star within a circle—to represent Earth. This usually takes the form of a wooden, stone or metal platter, upon which we place the bread that is passed around the circle

Coven chalices contain wine or juice to be shared in the circle.

Wands and athames are associated with Air and Fire, pentacles with Earth.

directly after the chalice. A little is broken off and eaten, then the loaf is passed on with a kiss and with the words: "May you never hunger" or "Blessed Be."

In most circles the wand is associated with Air, though in some traditions this symbolism is reversed with that of Fire. A wand can be used in much the same way as an athame—to direct energy. Wands take many forms; they are usually wooden but are sometimes made from quartz or copper. They vary from very simple polished wood to extremely elaborate, set with semi-precious stones and carved with magical symbols.

In circles that have an initiatory tradition, the cords are placed at the center. These are the shroud measures (circumference of head, around the heart and the exact height) of a witch and are magically linked with them. They are placed in the center of the circle as they are seen as the umbilical that links us to the realm of Spirit.

On a final note, traditionally, once a circle is cast, no one leaves it until it is dispersed, with the exception of an emergency. This is to retain the integrity of the sacred space within the cast circle.

how to cast a circle

Traditionally, the circle is cast with an athame.

Once the space is prepared (see pages 198–201), a circle can be cast. This involves opening up your energy points or chakras, in order to make yourself the conduit for the energy needed to cast a circle. The process by which you prepare yourself is identical to that offered as a guide to preparation for visualization on pages 138–139.

When you are fully prepared, and the flow of energy is established, concentrate on directing some of that energy via your solar plexus through your arms and out through your athame, wand or finger to draw a line in the air around the ritual space. It is easier to hold the visualized circle in the mind's eye if you start by visualizing a circle within the room in which you are working. As your confidence grows you can move on to casting circles that encompass the whole of the room in which you are working, transcending the visible boundaries of the walls, ceiling and floor.

Traditionally, one nods to the north and begins casting in the east, extending the arms to direct the energy outward and moving deosil. This is known as *describing* a circle. As you return to the starting point you should seal it with a few words, saying, for example: "I cast this circle as a boundary between the worlds; a container of the power I/we raise and a guardian and protector of all who stand within."

Welcome in the elements, beginning in the east and moving deosil. You may eventually generate your own form of welcome, but as a working guide, it is usual to name the qualities each element brings to the circle before lighting the appropriate candle in its honor: "In the east, the element of Air, bringing to this circle the gifts of clarity and communication, you are honored in this circle. Hail and welcome." It is usual, if working with a group, for all participants to repeat the last phrase.

At the end of a ritual, although practices vary, it is usual to thank the elements for their presence, saying: "Hail and farewell," and extinguish the candles, though traditionally the Spirit candle is kept alight until the last person leaves saying: "Hail and abide." The circle is then closed by the person who cast it, either by dispersing it outward into the Universe or drawing its energy back through the athame, finger or wand, to the body and into the Earth.

Rituals and spell-work

Although all spells are rituals, not all rituals are spells. Put simply, a ritual is an act that symbolizes or enacts something in token and is used to celebrate, commemorate or transform the object or event in question according to the will of the person(s) who carry it out. All of us have our own little everyday rituals—lighting the candles on a birthday cake, signing leaving cards for colleagues, throwing confetti or rice at weddings, wearing our own favorite scarves or shirts to sporting events or even touching wood for luck. When ritual

A ritual symbolizes or enacts the will of the witch in token.

Spells are seen as part of our spiritual practice.

takes place within the circle—within sacred space—it becomes especially charged with our intent, both because we raise energy and concentrate it within the circle before we release it into the web of existence, and because we conduct rituals with our deities as witnesses.

In this sense, all spells, acts undertaken in token in order to produce change in consensual reality, are actually rituals. It is true to say that all rituals are magical in their own way, but this does not make them spells. Some rituals are forms of celebration used to mark change rather than precipitate it; for example, Esbats or Moon circles which celebrate a particular phase of the Moon (see pages 230–233 and pages 366–381). We may carry out magical work and spells within it and, by participating, transform ourselves, but the ritual itself may still be primarily a marker. Some rituals celebrate, commemorate or initiate change, such as initiations, handfasting, namings or Sabbats (seasonal festivals) or may be a mixture and encompass all three functions.

Spells are rituals focused on a single intent and outcome. It is common for a circle to be cast just for the purpose of performing a single spell, then closed once it is completed. This tends to happen more often in solo work, though it is not unusual for a group to get together for a single, urgent spell. As a rule, it is not wise to perform more than three spells in the course of one circle, as spells take a good deal of energy and concentration (see pages 266–267) and humans tend to function best at a magical and psychological level in triplicities—as evidenced by the incidents of three that crop up in stories.

Rituals and spells undertaken in the spirit of honesty, compassion and a genuine desire for growth and knowledge are never wasted—and in Wicca they are seen as an integral part of our spiritual practice.

Timing of spells and rituals

When you come to practice spells and conduct rituals, you will learn that there are a number of conventions within Wicca based on what we call "correspondences." Working with correspondences means matching the nature of the work you are undertaking with the appropriate symbols, colors, deities, day of the week, phase of the moon or planetary hour. Wicca takes an approach to magic and ritual based on principles of sympathy—representing like with like—known as "sympathetic magic." In the bad old days where magicians and witches divided approaches to magic into high and low magic, this approach was classed within the low category. This was an unfortunate and misleading way of describing a highly developed tradition of tapping into deep-seated inner knowledge and power through systems of affinity symbols. It has well-rooted historical precedents and is the foundation of much of what was once classed, similarly inaccurately, as high magic—that which depends more heavily on its ceremonial and arcane aspects than its connection with natural knowledge.

Within this sympathetic approach, timing is an important part of planning and carrying out ritual and spell-work. In Wicca, we work with the phases of the Moon partly because of the changes in energy that occur in its cycle around the Earth and partly because of the doctrine of sympathy. This latter aspect sees the different phases chiefly as symbolic and so spells for increase, attraction and growth are generally cast on the waxing or growing cycle of the Moon, while spells for decrease, binding or banishing are cast on the waning or shrinking cycle of the Moon. In the northern hemisphere the waxing phase sees the crescent growing from a right-hand arc to a full disc, while the waning phase sees the full disc shrinking on the right-hand side to an arc on the left. When the Moon is entirely covered by Earth's shadow, it is said to be a "New" or "Dark" Moon. This phase is particularly good for beginning new projects and enhancing psychic protection. Full Moon is particularly good for celebratory rituals.

The phases of the Sun are also relevant in Wicca, mainly through its seasonal festivals. These are celebrated either on the day of the appropriate solstice or equinox, or in the case of the Celtic fire festivals, on the calendar date or the nearest Full Moon after the key events that mark it.

The days of the week have planetary correspondences as well as associated deities. This makes certain days particularly suitable for specific spells. Monday is associated with the Moon, for example, and is seen as particularly good for fertility, material growth and dream-work. It is also associated with lunar deities, and they bring their own particular flavor to ritual

Spells cast on a waning Moon are for depletion, banishing and repelling.

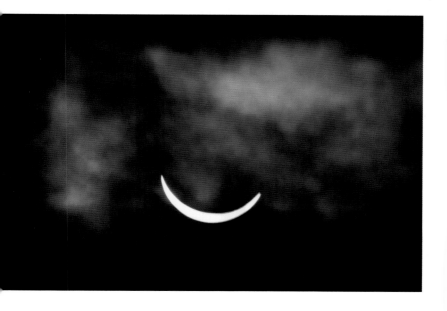

Astrological correspondences allow us to take into account particular influences.

or spell-work, according to which you choose. There are also astrological correspondences—for example, characteristics of certain signs that work well with particular elements in spells or rituals. Less frequently used are the planetary hours—each hour in the day is said to be ruled by a planetary influence, and some magicians time their spells almost to the minute by drawing in correspondences of Moon phase, the astrological sign of that Moon at a given time, and the appropriate planetary hour.

Most witches give primary importance to the Moon phase to guide them in their work for several reasons. The nature of Wiccan spirituality is such that our affinity to nature, with its changing cyclical energies, draws us to the Moon, our nearest celestial neighbor. We feel her in our tides, our biological cycles and in our dreams—at all levels, in fact. But there are historical and cultural reasons why witches favor the Moon phase above all other considerations in spiritual and magical work; for a long time primacy has been given to *logos*, the rational, left-brain functions. Witches envisage this changing to incorporate, as we do in our spiritual practices, elements of reflection, intuition, process and change—all of which we tend to associate with the Moon. This is not to say that we consider the Sun unimportant; simply that the Moon carries a particular significance for us.

Witches are also prepared, when need outweighs the principle of timing, to forgo tradition. The guiding principle, as ever, is to "Harm None" and if in order to stop or prevent harm we need to act quickly, then need, rather than convention and tradition, will direct our decisions.

Witches generally place the Moon phase above other considerations— except in urgent need.

Correspondences

The Five Elements Table

	Air	Fire
Spells	Communication, swiftness, exams, legal, knowledge and learning, conveyancing, travel	Defense, willpower, courage, inspiration
Herbs and plants	Lavender, eucalyptus, comfrey, wormwood, lilac	Rosemary, rue, dandelion, saffron, nettles, St. John's wort (*Hypericum*)
Trees	Birch, ash	Oak, rowan
Incenses and oils	Benzoin, sandalwood, lavender	Cinnamon, frankincense, vanilla, juniper
Astrological sign	Aquarius, Gemini, Libra	Aries, Leo, Sagittarius
Day of week	Wednesday	Tuesday, Thursday
Planet(s)	Mercury	Sun, Mars
Color	Yellow	Red
Metal	Mercury (quicksilver)	Tin
Symbol	Upward pointing triangle traversed, feather, incense	Upward pointing triangle, flame, blade, salamanders
Magical tool	Wand	Athame
Animal totems	All birds	Salamander, big cats
Body parts	Lungs, head	Heart
Direction	East	South

THE ELEMENTS

The table below is a working guide to commonly recognized correspondences.

Water	Earth	Spirit
Love, healing, dream-work, women's cycles, childbirth, emotional issues	Manifestation, material wealth, shelter, fertility, growth	Initiation, transition, transformation, spiritual growth and knowledge
Poppy, rose, myrtle, violet, valerian, lovage, chamomile, geranium, hyacinth	Patchouli, sage, mandrake, woodbine, horehound, pennyroyal	Gentian, lotus, belladonna*, henbane* (*poisonous)
Willow, apple	Cypress, pine	Elder, yew
Myrrh, rose absolute, orris root	Patchouli, pine resin, white sage, mandrake root	Nag champa, copal, dittany of Crete
Pisces, Cancer, Scorpio	Taurus, Virgo, Capricorn	
Monday, Friday	Saturday	Sunday
Moon, Venus, Neptune	Gaia, Saturn, Pluto	Uranus
Blue	Green	Purple, white
Silver, copper	Iron, lead	Gold
Downward pointing triangle, caldron, glass, mirror	Downward pointing triangle traversed, pentacle, wood, metal, stone, crystals, dragon	Upward pointing pentagram, terminated clear quartz, web, thread
Chalice	Pentacle	Cords
Fish, water-based mammals	Hare, wolf, bear, serpent	Spider
Womb, kidneys, bladder, liver	Bowels, spine	
West	North	Center

PLANETARY HOURS

The table below is based on time divisions between sunset and sunrise. This may differ in your locality according to the time of year, so to pinpoint the "hour" dedicated to the appropriate planet for a spell or ritual, calculate the number of minutes between sunset and sunrise, divide by 12 and number each unit one to 12. The planetary hour that corresponds to your needs indicates what time you need to conduct your work.

Note that the following column is a rough guide—more comprehensive systems have a rolling matrix that differs according to the days of the week. For simplicity's sake, however, the following offers an outline based on numerological and planetary correspondence.

planetary hours table

Planet	Hour
Sun	1
Moon	2
Mercury	3
Jupiter	4
Mars	5
Venus	6
Neptune	7
Pluto	8
Mercury	9
Jupiter	10
Uranus	11
Earth	12

Sample calculation

For example, you wish to cast a spell to help a friend who is having trouble concentrating on her studies.

- The best planet to work with is Mercury.
- Your local times are sunset 9.30 P.M., sunrise 4.30 A.M.
- The number of minutes between sunset and sunrise is 420, divided by 12 = 35 minutes.
- The first division of time after sunset ruled by Mercury is the third "hour:" 3 x 35 minutes = 105 minutes, 9.30 P.M. + 105 minutes = 11.15 P.M.

MOON SIGNS

It is now possible to download a reliable ephemeris, a table of predictions of planetary movements, from the Web, or in the appendices of good astrological guides. This will indicate when the Moon moves through different astrological signs and you will need to consult an ephemeris if you decide to work with the traditional correspondences outlined below. These indicate the best Moon-signs for different types of spell and are intended as an indicative guide, which you can add to as you progress in the Craft.

MOON SIGNS TABLE

Type of spell	Aries	Taurus	Gemini	Cancer	Leo	Virgo	Libra	Scorpio	Sagittarius	Capricorn	Aquarius	Pisces
Love/relationships			•	•			•				•	•
Healing/emotions			•	•			•	•			•	•
Wealth/increase		•			•	•			•	•		
Employment/commerce			•		•				•	•	•	
Banishing/binding	•			•		•		•				
Protection	•	•			•				•			
Fertility	•	•				•		•		•		•

DAYS OF THE WEEK

The following table, based on traditional Wiccan correspondences, can be extended as your studies in the Craft develop.

Days of the Week Table

	Monday	Tuesday	Wednesday
Planet	Moon	Mars	Mercury
Colors	Silver, pewter, white, grey	Red	Yellow
Deity	Selene, Nephtys, Artemis, Isis	Mars/Ares Tiew, Oya, Kali	Mercury/Hermes, Athene, Sarasvarti, Woden
Associations	Fertility, increase, dream-work	Defense, protection, inspiration, defeating obstacles, courage, sex, dance	Communication, learning, study, exams and tests, legal issues, travel, ideas, memory, science
Metal	Silver	Iron	Mercury
Symbolic object	Caldron	Arrow	Staff

Thursday	Friday	Saturday	Sunday
Jupiter	Venus	Saturn	Sun
Purple, dark blue	Green	Black or brown	Gold
Thor, Jove/Jupiter, Rhiannon, Juno, Laxmi	Venus/Aphrodite, Angus, Parvarti	Hecate, Nemesis, Saturn	Brighid, Apollo, Lugh, Belissama
Generosity, natural justice, expansion, property, wills, family matters	Love, affection, friendships, partnership, allurement, sexuality, beauty, art	Boundaries, binding, exorcism, discipline, reduction, protection, deflection	Health, happiness, contentment, music, poetry
Tin	Copper	Lead	Gold
Drum	Rose, star symbol	Chain, cords	Disc

Finding a circle name

The guided visualization outlined on pages 148–151 will help you identify a circle name. The following methods should be combined with this.

METHOD 1: NUMEROLOGY

Add together the numbers in your name in order to find your nominal number using the letters of the name by which you are known, and the numbers in your birth-date, as set out in the example below.

1	2	3	4	5	6	7	8	9
A	B	C	D	E	F	G	H	I
J	K	L	M	N	O	P	Q	R
S	T	U	V	W	X	Y	Z	

JOAN SMITH (born October 25 1970)

J O A N S M I T H 2 5 1 0 1 9 7 0
$1 + 6 + 1 + 5 + 1 + 4 + 9 + 2 + 8 + 2 + 5 + 1 + 0 + 1 + 9 + 7 + 0 = 62$
$6 + 2 = 8$

Your new name should match this number when calculated in the same way. Joan Smith, for example, has discovered an affinity with the Goddess Andraste.

A N D R A S T E
$1 + 5 + 4 + 9 + 1 + 1 + 2 + 5 = 28$
$2 + 8 = 10$
$1 + 0 = 1$

This does not match Joan's nominal number. However, if the name is altered slightly to ensure that it matches Joan's nominal number, this gives Joan an entirely new and possibly unique name:

A   N   D   R   A   S   E
1 + 5 + 4 + 9 + 1 + 1 + 5 = **26**
2 + 6 = **8**

METHOD 2:
MIX AND MATCH

Your circle-name expresses an aspect of your spiritual self.

Divide a clean piece of paper into four equal-sized sections. In each draw a natural object or symbol that represents how you see the following aspects of yourself: In the top left-hand section how you see yourself; in the top right-hand section how you deal with those close to you; in the bottom left-hand section how your friends see you; in the bottom right-hand section your inner, emotional and spiritual life. Let us suppose that you draw a waxing crescent Moon, a cat, a sprig of sage and an ash tree, respectively. Combining two of these symbols in any order gives you a list of possible names: Ash-Crescent/Moon, Sage-Cat, Moon-Sage etc. If you meditate further, you may find that one aspect of yourself comes to the fore, indicating a single name. For example, if it becomes important to you that your friends see you as wise—a sage, in fact, then you can take this herb name. This exercise is not an exact science but it can be a creative spur to finding your circle-name.

BECOMING
WICCAN

The Wiccan way

One of the most common questions asked of witches is "what do you mean by 'witch' exactly?" To be a witch means to work with nature, to honor the God and Goddess and to be a healer, both of self and of others. Witches have names for these different roles that unite in the word *witch*. Those who work with nature, who see the Spirit within all things and strive to make best use of

A witch is also a priest or priestess.

the cures and benefits that the natural world offers are the Wise. This is a very literal meaning of the word *witch*, whose linguistic roots tap into a meaning that combines knowledge and how to use it. We may not start out wise, but as an aspiration, it has its merits.

Being a Wise-woman or -man means treading lightly on the Earth and working toward environmental protection and sustainability. Witches do not simply mouth platitudes about healing the Earth; we do something about it, both in a local sense—recycling and shopping as ethically as we can—and in a wider global sense—active involvement in campaigns to halt pollution and deforestation.

Many witches are expert in alternative or complementary therapies such as herbal medicine, aromatherapy, homeopathy, acupuncture and reflexology. However, promoting the wellbeing of individuals is only one part of this role. The task of healing applies in a much wider sense; working for peace, justice and equality are as much a part of being a healer as the smaller acts we carry out for individuals.

Witches are magicians in the sense of casting spells, and in transforming our own lives, the lives of those who seek our help and society as a whole. We weave patterns in the great web to positively transform. When we work spells to this end, we are not being selfish or unspiritual—this is an integral part of our spiritual path, the Wiccan way.

The role that takes most people by surprise is that of the priest or priestess. This role means a commitment to honor whatever we perceive to be God or Goddess in the best way that we can. We do not rely on others to go between us and our god or goddess—we are our own priest or priestess. We do not mediate for others or claim higher spiritual authority over others, but we can offer service to the sick or incapacitated if they ask for our help.

Initiation and the degree system

Generally, to be initiated into an organization, group, or tradition is to be introduced to its patterns, laws and secrets, and aspects of this are present in initiation within Wicca. In spiritual terms, however, the act of initiation is more than simply having an induction into the Craft. It is an act of commitment to the Goddess—the patron of initiation—signaling to the great web that connects all things that you stand before the deities to dedicate yourself to the ways of the Wise. The old-fashioned way of describing this act was to say that its intention is to "draw the attention of the Godhead" to you. Whichever your tradition and whatever the variation on the ritual you end up with, the key purpose of initiation is to enter into a commitment to learn and signal your preparedness to become Wicca or wise.

Beyond this central factor, there are other purposes to initiation, some linked with community or group traditions. If you work in a group, that group will witness the dedication and promises you make within the circle—these are very sacred and binding undertakings. When you have joined them in this way, you become part of a community of people who have taken the same step; at that point you can be introduced to information and traditions that are held back until a witch is initiated into the mysteries. This may involve the people in your group offering their magical names or revealing the name of the coven, if these are withheld by custom until after initiation. It may also involve undertaking advanced training or being given particular coven responsibility.

Traditionally an acolyte approaches a group and works with them, or with members of the group, for a year and a day prior to initiation. Many groups are happy for new members to be involved in Sabbats (seasonal festivals) and Esbats (Moon circles) from the beginning, whereas others may restrict full circle involvement until after initiation. This is partly because the notion of initiation itself may differ slightly between groups and different traditions within Wicca.

For some, the ritual is carried out to precipitate spiritual changes, whereas for others it is to celebrate changes that have already been experienced and to mark this by making a commitment in front of Wiccan community and before the God or Goddess.

Some English Traditional Craft covens, particularly those following the Alexandrian tradition, have a tripartite degree system of initiation. The first

Some initiatory traditions have ancient antecedents.

initiation is as witch and priest/priestess, and is considered to be overseen by the Goddess; the second, a year and a day later, is as mage and considered to be the domain of the God; while the third is initiation as high priest/priestess and involves the sacred conjunction of God and Goddess. It is not unknown for the second and third degree initiations to be undertaken together. After the third initiation as high priest/priestess, the initiate is considered ready to lead their own coven. For many Wiccan groups, however, one initiation is considered enough, and the mission is accomplished with one ceremony.

There was some debate in the Wiccan community several years ago about whether one could be considered "properly" initiated unless certain conditions were met. This discussion involved the issue of gender polarity—the complementary energy of male-to-female and female-to-male initiation. This was really only of interest to those groups who insisted on working with this rather outmoded orthodoxy of "masculine/feminine" divides, but it did lead some members to claim that unless initiation had taken place according to this system, it was not a "proper" initiation and the person involved could not be considered a witch! Similarly, the opinion that only those who were initiated by another could be considered properly initiated got an airing. Both ideas are, of course, nonsense, so feel free to ignore them.

Self-initiation—going into the circle alone to dedicate yourself to the Goddess and to pledge an oath to be willing to learn the ways of the Wise—is valid initiation. It is very different from group-led initiation, certainly, but it is no less genuine, heartfelt or successful for that. The key relationship in initiation is that between the initiate and the Goddess—not between the initiate and the human agency of that initiation.

If you are considering initiation with a group of people you work with and trust, do check whether they consider initiation to be "into the Craft" or "into the group," in case you are working at cross purposes. Many groups consider initiation into the Craft by their group to be an implicit acceptance and welcome into the group, but some do not and it is best to check how the other people you are working with actually see it.

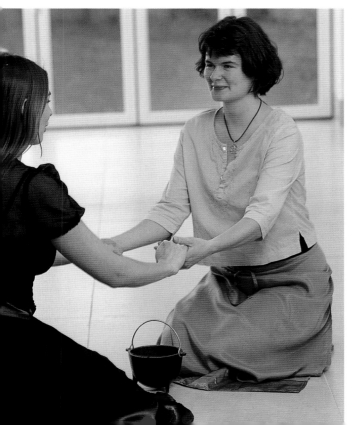

Group-workings can amplify the energy raised for spell-work.

Initiation ceremony

The exact outline of an initiation ceremony differs between traditions, groups and individuals. However, some key elements are common to all initiation ceremonies and to this end it is possible to describe one here. There are some elements of initiation that cannot be outlined publicly, however, not because they cannot be revealed on pain of death or curse, nor because they are somehow morally suspect, but because there are some aspects of initiation that need to be kept aside for the occasion.

Although on the whole one should know in advance exactly what to expect of a ritual, there is an exception in one's own initiation. It may be, for example, that the exact question you are posed as you enter the circle (see page 228) is not known to you beforehand. Working out the answer in advance does not promote the same sense of immediacy produced by this "surprise" element, and neither does it allow you to become emotionally and intellectually vulnerable before the Goddess in the way that you need to be. If you are working with sensible and kind people, there is nothing to fear from the odd surprise element being included in your initiation.

I should stress, however, that this trust should be given only to people whom you know and trust, and with whom you have worked for some time; the year and a day rule is good guidance here. Sexual activity is generally not a part of initiation until third degree in the Alexandrian tradition, and even then it is generally between a committed couple entering initiation together, or done "in token"; the "Sacred Marriage" is enacted symbolically with a chalice and athame, and not between persons. If you find anyone trying to convince you that initiation involves sex with them, steer clear and alert sensible people you can trust within the Wiccan community. Somebody who so disregards the meaning of Wicca cannot possibly have the sort of knowledge and spirit you need to guide you through initiation.

With all group initiations, the circle is cast and the elements are welcomed before the initiate is conducted to the circle. It is usual for initiations to be carried out sky-clad, or naked. This symbolizes your willingness to stand before the Goddess as you came into the world, without pretention or trappings, and is in imitation of the journey of the Goddess to the Underworld, where she gained knowledge of the mysteries of death. The initiate is blindfolded and may be

We enter the Craft in love and in trust.

loosely bound with cords of their measure (their exact height, head circumference, and distance around their heart) from one ankle to the wrists. He or she is led to a gateway cut in the circle where a priest or priestess stands at the threshold to ask for the passwords and issue a challenge. The passwords are simply "perfect love and perfect trust." The challenge will be a posed question, however, and it is rare for an initiate to be told what this is beforehand.

In Wicca, the initiator kneels before the initiate.

When the initiate crosses the threshold into the circle, he or she is led to the center where more questions may be posed, one of which will be the initiate's circle-name. The initiate will be instructed in what it means to be a witch and priest/priestess by one of their initiators and will kneel—for the first and last time ever—before the Goddess. The initiate is asked if they are willing to suffer to learn and, depending on the answer, will be offered the oath they are asked to swear in fealty to their brothers and sisters in the Craft. Afterwards, they are introduced, still blindfolded, to the elements Air, Fire, Water and Earth (Spirit is present in the cords that bind them). The initiate is offered the five-fold kiss, which may take the form of anointing with perfumed oil rather than a physical kiss. This involves the initiator kneeling before the initiate and kissing or anointing them on five places on the body, blessing each respectively:

> *Blessed be thy feet that walk in the sacred ways*
> *Blessed be thy knees that have knelt before the Goddess*
> *Blessed be thy womb/phallus without which we could not be*
> *Blessed be thy breast created in beauty*
> *Blessed be thy lips which will speak the sacred names.*

At this point the blindfold may be removed and the initiate is introduced to those present by their circle-names and welcomed into the Craft and, as appropriate, into the coven. In some cases, customs, traditions or stories may be related to the newly born witch, and some groups offer the new witch a gift or have a celebration.

This description is of a typical coven-led initiation. There are variations between groups and traditions, and between individuals where initiation is undertaken as a solo act. But its key ingredient is the act of commitment to the ways of the Wise and a willingness to learn.

Covens and coven work

A coven will generally meet together for Full-Moon circles or other Moon-phase celebrations—Esbats—and celebrate the Sabbats together. Some old-fashioned covens still have a high priest or priestess, though many now pass this office around the more experienced members of the group or dispense with it altogether if the group is organized in a non-hierarchical fashion.

There are many benefits to belonging to a group, not least the range of abilities, knowledge and advice on hand to a relative newcomer. Often you will find that each member, though possessing a fair range of knowledge in the Craft, will have a particular expertise of their own. Other members of the group may turn to them for advice on their specialty. This does not mean that they are seen only as "the herbalist," "the astrologer" or "the Craft authority"; most witches are so curious about different aspects of the Craft that each witch has more than one area of expertise!

In circle-work members have different roles—for example, one officer for each of the

Group-work involves sharing our gifts and knowledge.

element quarters—that are rotated for each circle. Sometimes the roles allotted or chosen have to do with the stage of that person's learning in the Craft. In some cases roles are selected by lottery. Some covens have coordinators who advise people what needs to be done and organize how this will happen, rather than telling others what to do.

Covens are about commitment and building commonality with the energy of those with whom you raise power and work ritual and magic. You do become used to each other's vibe the longer you work with someone, and this development is sometimes described as a "group mind." This means joining yourself with the whole rather than surrendering your own individuality to that of the group; the covens that work best are those in which people want to turn up for every meeting rather than feeling brow-beaten by others into doing so.

There is no room for ego within a coven, because we are all learning until the day we die, and the truly wise know or at least begin to see this by the time they are working within a group. Given that Wicca is the religion where the initiator kneels before the initiate and not vice versa, it should be obvious that witches approach learning in a very particular way. We accept that however experienced we are, there is always something new to learn; often we learn more from those to whom we offer our knowledge and experience than they learn from us.

The reason that some witches like to work with others is found in the Mother Charge, which is spoken by a chosen priest or priestess at the opening of an Esbat to remind us of who the Goddess is and who we are. Those of us who prefer to work with other witches feel the full power of this Charge when it is recited in the presence of our sisters and brothers in the Craft. It confirms us as a faith community, reminds us that we are not alone and that when we join together, we are joined by the Goddess herself. For some witches, being committed to a coven and working in companionship and mutual support with others reminds us of the ideals to which we aspire.

the mother charge

Whenever you have need of me, once in the month when the Moon is full, meet together and adore me, for I am the Queen of all Witchery. Assemble there all you who would learn; to you I will teach things that are yet unknown. You shall be free from all slavery and as a sign that you are free you shall be joyful in your rites...for mine is the ecstasy of the spirit and mine is joy on Earth, for my law is love unto all beings...

...Keep pure your highest ideals and let nothing stop you or turn you aside. Mine is the secret door which opens upon the door of youth and mine is the cup of life, the Caldron of Cerridwen which is the Grail of Immortality...

...I am the Goddess who gives the gift of joy to the mortal heart. Upon Earth I give knowledge of the eternal Spirit and beyond death I give peace and freedom and reunion with those who have gone before. Nor do I demand sacrifice for I am the Mother of all living and my love is poured out upon the Earth.

Coven organization

It is usual for covens to meet for circle-work at least once a month for Esbats. When a Sabbat falls within a Moon cycle, it will generally meet twice in that month. However, if the Sabbat falls on a Full Moon, some groups forgo the Esbat for that cycle. Larger covens may also make separate arrangements to accommodate circle-work outside of the main group as training sessions for newcomers. It is common for covens to be called together to do adhoc healing work or when there is a crisis or an emergency involving a group member. In general, if you are working with a coven, you could expect to be undertaking circle-work with them on average once every two weeks. This is, of course, only a rough working guide—the preferences and practices of different covens will vary considerably.

Esbats are traditionally Full-Moon circles. Covens generally adhere to this, though some like to celebrate different phases of the Moon together occasionally. The main purpose of group Esbats is to celebrate and honor the deities, to work toward spiritual development, to develop magical and ritual skills, and to raise energy together to cast spells. See the box (right) for an outline of a typical Esbat.

A typical esbat

- Meditation/opening chakras
- Cleansing ritual space with salt and water
- Casting the circle
- Welcoming the elements and lighting candles
- The Mother Charge/statement of intent/welcome to the Esbat
- Readings/show and tell on season/phase of Moon
- Guided visualization/ developmental work
- Raising energy, spell-casting
- Cakes and ale
- Thank elements
- Disperse circle

Preparing sacred space helps us to get ready for a ritual.

The Sabbats follow a roughly similar outline, but add an element of ritual associated with the season itself: For example, maypole dancing at Beltane. It is usual for energy raised at a Sabbat to be directed toward those who have requested healing rather than toward specific magical spells. The latter are usually undertaken at Esbats or at circles called specifically for that purpose.

The offices and roles for all types of rituals are decided in advance, and consequently most covens have organizational meetings in addition to circle-based gatherings. As discussed earlier, there are various ways of allotting roles, but these are generally rotated between members of the circle.

Coven members may carry out solo circle-work for self-development and for spells in addition to the group circles. Sometimes two or three members may elect to work together occasionally or even routinely outside of coven gatherings. Others elect to work with non-coven members—and this is perfectly okay. What coven work should never do is restrict your own circle-work to coven meetings only—your commitment is to meet and work with the coven at given, agreed times; this does not give the coven exclusive rights to you.

Coven membership revolves around consent, discretion and confidentiality.

What is very important, however, is that your coven should be able to trust you with confidential issues that concern the group. This means not revealing anything about coven-work to those outside, including naming those who belong to your group. Although things are getting better for pagans and witches in some parts of the world, witches are not always happy with others knowing their business. No one should consider themselves in a position to judge whether another witch would like you to reveal their religion or practices to others without their express permission. Keeping coven business quiet is part of discretion and knowing when to stay silent. Apart from anything else, running around boasting, even to other witches, what your coven did last week is likely to dissipate the power of whatever you managed to put together, as well as seriously annoy your co-coveners!

Covens are about consensual membership and that consent extends beyond the initial decision to join. You can leave at any time you wish, but you are bound by an expectation of discretion and confidentiality in the same way as you are when you are a member. The exception, obviously, is where you have serious concerns about some of their practices from an ethical view, in which case speak to a trustworthy and respected member of the Wiccan community for advice. It was once the custom for a coven to retain the "measures" of a witch at initiation in order to ensure their silence. This dates back to the fearful times when betrayal could mean imprisonment or even torture and death to others. Because the measure is so intimately bound up with the witch's spirit, no witch would want to wrongfoot someone who possessed something that could be used against them magically. Nowadays covens give the measure back to the initiate and usually add the words: "You are free to leave if your heart leads you." Leave a coven if you feel that it is time to do so with a good heart and on good terms. You are entitled to do so without reproach.

Coven cooking

It is important to eat something after circles even if it is just a sip of juice and bite of bread passed around when it is time for "cakes and ale." But if your group is lucky enough to have kitchen facilities or a place to set up some food for afterward, a communal post-circle meal can be very sociable! You can develop your own repertoire by researching which foodstuffs are associated with particular festivals, but the following recipes will get you started. The stew is good for cooking in a large pot over an open fire if you are on a campout together.

mooncakes

Makes up to 24 cookies

Ingredients

- 4 oz (125 g) soya margarine
- 2–3 oz (50–75 g) Demerara sugar
- 3 drops pure vanilla essence
- 4 oz (125 g) plain uncooked oatmeal
- 4 oz (125 g) wholemeal flour
- a little soya milk to moisten

Method

1 Mix the margarine to a smooth paste, adding the sugar and vanilla.

2 Blend in the oats and add the flour gradually, moistening slightly with soya milk to make a stiff dough.

3 Flour the work surface and rolling-pin, then roll out the dough to a thickness of approximately ¼ inches (5 mm).

4 Using a crescent-shaped cookie cutter, cut out 24 cookies; place on a greased and floured tin, then cook in a preheated oven at 350°F (180°C), Gas Mark 4 until firm and golden, 12–15 minutes.

5 Cool completely before storing.

cIRCLe STeW

To satisfy very hungry coveners, serve this stew with couscous, rice or large chunks of wholemeal bread.

Serves up to 13

Ingredients

- 2 tablespoons (30 ml) olive oil
- 10 large garlic cloves, finely chopped
- 5 large onions, finely chopped
- 10 cinnamon sticks
- 1 teaspoon medium chilli powder
- 4 heaped teaspoons turmeric
- 8 large carrots, chopped
- 8 large parsnips, sliced
- 8 large potatoes, chopped into eight pieces each
- 6 lbs (2.7 kilos) tomatoes, chopped
- 3 heaped tablespoons tomato purée
- 3½ pints (2.1 litres) stock made with vegan stock cubes
- 1 level teaspoon low-sodium salt
- 8 large courgettes/zucchini, thickly sliced
- 1½ lbs (675 g) field mushrooms, chopped

Method

1 Heat the oil in a heavy-bottomed casserole, then gently soften the garlic and onion and add the spices.

2 When the onions are translucent, add the chopped carrots, parsnips and potatoes, stirring to ensure that they do not stick to the pan.

3 Add the tomatoes, tomato purée, stock and salt.

4 Bring to the boil, cover and simmer for 20 minutes or until the carrots are cooked.

5 Add the courgettes and mushrooms and continue to cook for another 10 minutes.

Working with fire

Fire is used in group circle-work in the form of candles that we light to honor the elements, the candles and lamps that grace our altars and those we use generally to light the ritual space. We also use incense sticks and cones, or charcoal discs on which to scatter blended loose incense. It is important, therefore, to ensure that coveners are safety-conscious.

It is a good idea to keep a fire blanket and a hand-held extinguisher in the ritual room. It is rare that such measures are needed, but it is better to be prepared than to risk dangerous accidents. If your coven works indoors, you should all agree on actions to take in the case of an emergency. This should include safe evacuation of everyone in the building and knowing the best exit points. If

Candles should always burn down under supervision.

doors are locked during a ritual, ensure that everyone knows where the keys are. If you wear robes for ritual, make sure that these are not highly flammable, and watch out for sleeves and hems near candle-flames.

Much spell-work involves the use of candles. One method of using fire in spell-work is to anoint a candle with consecrated oil from bottom to top, top to bottom, then bottom to halfway up. While doing so, you should think about the intent of your spell. When the candle is lit, it melts away the wax, releasing into the great web all the energy and intent that you have placed in the candle.

Another method for using fire as part of spell-work is to have a balefire, a sacred fire. If you are working outside you may choose to burn natural materials and to dig a fire pit, keeping a bucket of sand or water near by for safety.

Alternately, if you have the use of a large iron caldron you can set a fire in it, raising it off the ground onto large stones. If you blend a mixture half pure alcohol, half Epsom salts, this produces a beautiful blue flame. If you have something you wish to be rid of—a bad habit, for instance—you can write this on a piece of paper, fold it up, concentrate on expelling the habit and throw it into the fire. A more dramatic effect can be achieved by using an icecube to represent something you wish to be rid of—throw it into the flames and see what happens!

Fire is a useful tool in spell-work.

magic

how magic works

Working with magic for years will give you a clearer understanding of the Craft than reading about it in a book. I have been casting spells for decades and experience has deepened my feel for magic. Sometimes I can sense intuitively whether a spell has "taken" while I am casting it, and, on occasion, some time after I will see the individual threads coming together in everyday events. However, I am still delighted by new realizations about the way that magic works and I expect I shall continue to be until I pass to the Summerlands! There are a number of theories on how magic works, and you may find these useful to know about and test out for yourself.

Many witches believe that the whole of existence is connected together. This connection is visualized as a many-dimensional web, the threads of which form part of the mystery of the element of Spirit, which is the connecting force. The best way to understand this is to imagine Spirit as the connecting feature of a web—the node where different threads are held together in

Magic comes from ancient traditions, written and verbal.

a pattern. The thread is the physical part of the web, but it would not be a web at all were it not for the way in which the threads are woven together. Although the thread is palpable and can be physically experienced whether or not it is part of a web, a connection—the part that is so essentially Spirit—cannot. This does not make it less real; indeed, it can be said to be the defining aspect of the web. This is how we see magic.

To cast a spell within this worldview is to weave a new pattern into the web. When we work ritual, we are working with nature, weaving into the flow a pattern which further along will produce change. Many of us call ourselves "patterners," which makes it easier to understand how we approach such things as spell-casting and divination. These activities are apparently at opposite ends of the patterning process: The former for creating and the latter for reading patterns. However, they are interconnected.

We "tap into" the web in order to effect change by using symbols to send signals to our deeper selves—the self that is most knowledgeable and acquainted with Spirit and the God or Goddess. We work in the circle, the sacred space between the worlds, to draw in threads from the great web and work them according to our will before sending them back out into the ether with another pattern in the mix.

Some magicians take the view that magic is about effecting change in accordance with the will—a view advanced by Aleister Crowley, an early twentieth-century magician. However, the majority of us who work with magic on a regular basis and in accordance with Wiccan ethics feel that we cause changes in consciousness according to our will—a theory originally put forward by Dion Fortune, an eminent and influential British occultist and a contemporary of Crowley. The issue of changes in consciousness is a vital aspect of working magic and ritual.

When we go into the circle to work magic we need to prepare ourselves. This involves leaving aside the distractions of everyday worries that have a call on our attention. It does not require us to leave behind all our workaday worries; simply that we ensure that they are not distracting us from the task in hand. This is why a group spends time in preparation before circle-work, shedding the masks and burdens we wear and carry in the outside world, and activating our energy points. We prepare to change our state of consciousness in order to walk between the worlds, weave our patterns and send them out onto the great web. We need to change ourselves before we can change anything in the world around us, and the more we do this, the more we can enter this state at will.

As you become more adept at working magic and spell-casting, you will recognize the different levels of energy in the circle and the way that they alter in the course of a ritual. Changes wrought by magical acts, when manifested, play their own part in changing consciousness, and so the cycle of change continues; you will come to identify this as you grow in experience.

A group focuses on a spell in preparation.

Principles, laws and ethics

In magic there is a principle known as the Law of Threefold Return. This belief says that whatever you send out is returned to you threefold. In fact, this is just a poetic way of saying that your actions will return to you—for good or bad, and that you need to think before you act. This principle is often quoted for the benefit of journalists and their reading public as a way of dispelling myths about those who "abuse" their power to send out curses. After all, why would a witch send out something nasty if it was going to revisit itself upon him or her three times more powerfully than when it was sent out? It is a commonsense way of alerting people to the consequences of their actions and reminding them to pause before deciding what is really needed. It is not a hard and fast law that what you send out comes back literally threefold—when I give a bunch of flowers to someone I don't receive three bunches back! However, kind acts make the world kinder, even by a miniscule amount, and that is returned to me if only in the sense that knowing kindness can make a difference makes a better world possible. In short, the law of return is a spiritual truth and an ethical guideline.

There seem to be a number of laws knocking about on the occult circuit, each of which claim to be the definitive three, seven or nine laws of magic. Firstly they are not definitive, secondly, some of them are nonsense, and thirdly, the most sensible of them amount to the same thing: Harm None. You cannot change the will of another by magic and neither should you try. The only will you can work on is your own. Witches tend to listen and ask questions of the person seeking magical help, then they ask questions of themselves, before acting. We listen and ask in order to establish exactly what is needed. A person asking us to curse their cruel boss will be advised to approach their union for practical and legal help, and be offered healing work to help deal with the effect that bullying is having on them.

We ask ourselves whether what we are asking for through magic is strictly needful—this isn't such a bad guideline to work within.

A witch directs energy to cast her circle.

Popular spells

Humans don't come with feeding and care instructions attached but we do come with a few basic needs. We need shelter, food, warmth, health, a purpose in life and love. The most commonly requested spells in the annals of magic roughly reflect this and in the remainder of this section of the book you will find spells that represent these very human requirements.

At the top of the list of the most popular spells are those to do with love and vengeance. In both cases, we carefully explain to the supplicants exactly why we can't give them what they want, and then offer them another way of looking at their situations. In the case of love, we cannot direct our magic toward a particular person, we cannot affect the free will of another, nor would we. If the

Listening carefully to a supplicant and asking the right questions gets us nearer to the root of what is needed.

Love spells are among the most popular requests put to witches.

supplicant is ready for love to come into their lives, then the spell on pages 254–255 is the answer. If they are obsessed with a particular person because they feel that person's regard will validate them in some way, the problem is one of low self-esteem. In this case, the best thing to do is to work on the supplicant's sense of selfhood, and this may involve a little healing (see pages 252–253).

There are various methods for working magic. You will find advice on these on pages 266–267 and 270–277. All spells in this section are based on sympathetic magic—like representing like through the use of symbols—the most common kind used in Wicca. Before embarking on any of the spells, you are strongly advised to follow the advice given on pages 268–269 which deals with one popular method of preparation for ritual and magical work, aspects of which have already been explored in Visualization, particularly pages 138–139.

The spells are written as though a single person is performing them but can easily be adapted for group-work. All spells should be performed inside a cast circle with the elements welcomed prior to beginning your work. After all spell-work, close the sacral to third-eye chakras, leaving the base of spine and crown chakras very slightly open. Eat and drink in order to help consciously ground yourself and return to your everyday state of consciousness. All candles should be allowed to burn down completely under supervision unless otherwise stated.

healing spell

Healing takes many forms and applies itself to many purposes, but be clear that healing magic is not about curing terminal diseases or performing miracles; remember we are working with the flow, not against it. If those suffering with terminal or chronic illnesses feel that they will benefit from having strength, calm and tranquillity sent to them, then this is the healing that we can send. Sometimes spells do have remarkable results, but the truth is that we cannot change some things; but if we can offer other things that are needed, then we do.

spell

Timing

As this spell is for healing, work on a waxing or Full Moon. Sunday, ruled by the Sun, is the most auspicious day but give priority to the Moon phase.

Preparation

Prior to casting this spell, try to identify exactly what is needed. Pinpoint it to its simplest expression so that you can concentrate on the core issue and focus the energy where it is needed most.

You will need

- Blue candle, 8 inches (20 cm) in length
- Matches
- Fine paintbrush
- Small square plain paper
- Dot of red watercolor paint
- Small bowl of water

Casting the spell

1 Light the candle, saying: "Welcome, element of Water, patron of healing and cleansing. Witness and empower the changes I weave in your name."

2 Paint a red X on the centre of the paper, saying: "I name thee [name]'s pain/fear/anxiety."

3 Hold the paper before you in both hands and focus on the X. Imagine the supplicant's problem encapsulated inside that symbol.

4 Now place the paper in the bowl of water and move it around so that the paint disperses in the water and chant: "I wash away this pain's offence. Be ye gone and get ye hence!"

5 When the X is a pale smudge, remove the paper, crumple it up and throw it away.

6 Pour the water into the Earth immediately after the circle, saying: "So mote it be!"

Love spell

This spell is suitable for those who are ready for love to come to them. It signals that the supplicant is at a place in their lives where a loving relationship is desirable. It is most effective if the person asking for a new love carries out the spell for themselves. Otherwise, it is perfectly acceptable to cast this spell for someone else, provided that you are convinced that they are prepared to trust their wish to Spirit. Either way, it is necessary for the person asking for magical help to supply the crystals in this spell.

spell

Timing

Cast this spell on a waxing Moon, preferably on a Friday, ruled by lovely Venus.

Preparation

Leave the water for this spell out in the moonlight prior to casting the circle. In magic the Moon is a patron of the tides and this spell asks that a lover comes to the supplicant at the right time.

You will need

- Red candle, 8 inches (20 cm) in length
- Matches
- Small tumbled rose quartz
- Small tumbled clear quartz
- Chalice or glass
- Water, 4 fl oz (125 ml)
- Red cloth, 4 inches (25 cm) square
- Cord, 24 inches (60 cm) in length

Casting the spell

1 Light the red candle saying: "Passion burn bright like the Moon above me that I will meet with one who will love me."

2 Hold the rose quartz in one hand and the clear quartz in the other and visualize yourself walking on a seashore. A new love walks out of the waves toward you. As you walk toward each other, bring your hands together and transfer the clear stone to the hand holding the rose quartz.

3 Place the stones in the chalice and pour in the water, saying: "May the light of the Moon bring the gift I desire. Washed in by the tide and blessed by the fire."

4 This fire is the candle flame which should be allowed to burn down completely.

5 Leave the stones in the chalice for three days, remove them and place together in the red cloth which should be tied tightly into a pouch with the cord and worn about your neck for one moon cycle.

Wealth and weal spell

These days there is a tendency to see wealth as having more money than you could ever spend. However, wealth in ancient societies carried a slightly different meaning and one that we would do well to learn from; it meant having sufficient for your needs. The term *weal*, from which *wealth* is derived, referred to the yield of the land that accrued to the one that cultivated it. In a modern sense, *Wealth* and *weal* imply material things that are needful and the capacity by which to ensure them. If you are considering casting this spell, do ensure that what you are asking for is needful.

spell

Timing

Cast on a waxing Moon for gain, and on a Thursday, ruled by generous Jupiter.

Preparation

Note especially in the case of spells for wealth that enchantments (for this is the method for this spell) tend to work best if you focus on the outcome only and leave the method to the wonders of the web of magic. Try to focus on the results you wish to achieve and do not be tempted to speculate on how this will come about.

You will need

- Green candle, 8 inches (20 cm) in length
- Matches
- Bread, pea-sized crumb
- Milk, 3 drops
- Sugar, 1 teaspoon
- Disused spider's web
- Saucer

Casting the spell

1 Light the candle, saying: "Goddess of the Earth, Goddess of the Hearth, I plant this spell to bring forth Wealth."

2 Allow the bread to soak up the milk, then roll it in sugar and place inside the web.

3 Holding the bread and the web in your cupped hands, visualize the desired outcome while chanting: "Silver of Moon, Gold of Sun, cast the spell and be it done."

4 When you feel that you have thoroughly chanted your desire into the bread, sugar, milk and web, place them in the saucer.

5 Allow the candle to burn down completely in safety, then bury the mixture in Earth—preferably in your garden or window-box, as soon as possible the next day.

Employment or promotion spell

This versatile spell can be used for gaining employment or moving ahead if you already have a job. It can also be used if you are applying to go to college or university or for gaining voluntary work which interests you. It calls upon Air, the element of communication, since gaining advancement often depends on how well you articulate your abilities and aspirations. Naturally, this spell assumes that you are qualified for the posts or promotion for which you are applying; magic cannot give you something which you have not been prepared to work toward.

spell

Timing

Cast on the waxing Moon to bring you your desire, and work on Wednesday, dedicated to Mercury the planet of communication.

Preparation

You will notice a caveat in this spell: "An it harm none." Although this is an assumption for all spell-work, it is explicitly stated here to emphasize that you choose the right post at the right time, suited both to you and to those with whom you will be working.

You will need

- Yellow candle, 8 inches (20 cm) in length
- Matches
- Charcoal disk
- Fireproof dish
- Benzoin gum, ½ teaspoon

- Lavender seeds, ½ teaspoon
- Sycamore keys, 3

Casting the spell

1 Light the candle, saying: "Mercury, fleet and swift, witness and empower my wish."

2 Light the charcoal disc in the fireproof dish and when it is red-hot,

place the benzoin gum on it, saying: "Bring success an it harm none."

3 Next, sprinkle the lavender onto the dish, saying: "Carry my wish an it harm none."

4 Press the sycamore keys between your palms and visualize your desired outcome. Take a deep breath, summoning your will into it and exhale completely onto the keys.

5 Place the keys on the disk and allow them to burn completely.

6 Before dawn the next day, bury the cooled ashes beneath a flourishing tree or a potted plant.

Fertility spell

As midwives and as layers-out of the dead, the Wise-woman or Cunning-man of a tribe or village were intimately connected with key physical rites of passage. Witches are still asked for charms and spells to promote reproductive fertility. Fertility takes many forms outside of pregnancy. This spell focuses specifically on helping a couple conceive—it must be emphasized that this applies to cases where there are no physical reasons why a couple are not conceiving—but it may be adjusted to focus on fertility in other areas, such as a blessing for crops, a garden or a project.

spell

Timing

The best Moon phases are the waxing or Full Moon for fertility and growth; and the best day is Monday as its patron, the Moon, rules matters of pregnancy and childbirth.

Preparation

Work this spell outdoors in a green field, preferably shortly after dawn; for safety's sake you may wish to take along a friend to watch and ensure you are undisturbed.

You will need

- Tea-light, white or green
- Needle
- Matches
- Clean jar
- Ripe corn, 9 ears
- Patchouli essential oil, 3 drops
- Green cloth, 4 inches (10 cm) square
- Black cord, 24 inches (60 cm) in length

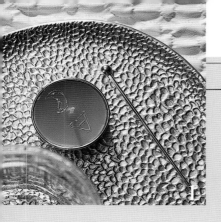

Casting the spell

1 Using the needle, inscribe into the surface of the tea-light a downward-pointing triangle traversed halfway through by a horizontal line, while saying: "Goddess of Earth, hold seeds of a birth."

2 Now inscribe a waxing crescent moon, saying: "Goddess of the Moon, swell the grain soon." Light the candle and place it in the jar.

3 Facing the Sun, hold up the corn in your cupped hands, saying: "Goddess of Fire, warm this desire."

4 Place the corn in the center of the cloth and anoint with the patchouli oil. Bring the corners of cloth together and fasten into a pouch with the cord. Place the pouch in the center of your circle and dance or walk around it nine times deosil; if you have mobility problems chant the three lines above three times each.

5 Give the pouch to the woman who desires the pregnancy to wear every night for the next three moons.

Protection spell

Sometimes we need to feel safe and shielded from the illwill, envy or hatred of other people. Because part of opening up to the Craft makes us sensitive to the atmosphere or energy that this can generate, it is good to renew our protection on a regular basis. This is not to keep the world out—dealing with sometimes unpleasant situations and people is a part of life—but a protective shield can function to filter out the worst of the bad emotions that dysfunctional people may direct toward us. If we do not shield ourselves to some extent we would soak up the depression, pessimism, and negativity and become unwell. This spell is a suitable antidote to that tendency.

spell

Timing

Cast this spell on a Dark Moon and on a Saturday, ruled by ringed Saturn.

Preparation

Prior to casting the circle, ensure that the charcoal is lit in the fireproof dish. Blend together the carrier oil and the cypress essential oil.

You will need

- Charcoal disc
- Fireproof dish
- Carrier oil, 1 teaspoon
- Cypress essential oil, 3 drops
- Black candle, 8 inches (20 cm) in length
- Matches
- Dried juniper berries, 8
- Salt in single-holed dispenser

Casting the spell

1 Anoint the candle with the blended oil, rubbing first bottom to top, then top to bottom, then bottom toward top, stopping halfway up.

2 Light the candle, saying: "Lilith of the Dark Moon, Hecate at the crossroads, Kali at the threshold."

3 Place the berries on the red-hot charcoal. Pour a single ring of salt on to the floor around yourself, the candle and the incense, saying: "I stand within protection of the Triple Goddess."

4 Place your power hand (writing hand) on your heart and say: "The protection of the Triple Goddess resides within me."

5 Sit down inside the salt circle, concentrate on the candleflame and visualize a shield of protection within and around you until you feel safe and confident. Blow away the salt circle with your breath and allow the candle to burn down safely.

Banishing spell

A banishing spell is not about making people disappear, although it might be tempting to fantasize that we could do this when someone is causing us distress. It is about dispelling bad behavior and replacing it with a more appropriate quality. You need to give serious thought to the consequences before casting this spell. Whatever is banished must be replaced; magic abhors a vacuum; unless bad behavior is replaced with something constructive, the person concerned will continue to be destructive.

spell

Timing

The best time for this spell is a waning Moon and the best day a Saturday, ruled by disciplinarian Saturn.

Preparation

If carrying out this spell on behalf of another, consider doing some healing work with that individual. Reassure them that in doing so you are not implying that the fault lies with them.

You will need

- Black candle, 8 inches (20 cm) in length
- Matches
- Hair or signature of perpetrator
- Plain paper, 2 inches (5 cm) square
- Pure alcohol, 1 teaspoon
- Epsom salts, 1 teaspoon
- Fireproof dish

- Heatproof mat
- Flower bulb, compost and pot

Casting the spell

1 Light the candle, saying: "Old One, Wise One, Slow but sure One, Guide my spell and be it done."

2 Hold up hair or signature, saying: "I name thee [name]'s power." Then wrap it in the paper and fold three times.

3 Place Epsom salts and alcohol in the fireproof dish (which you have placed on the heatproof mat) and light. Holding the folded paper say: "As this Moon shrinks to bone, this spell shall burn your power down." Throw the paper into the flame.

4 Hold the bulb before the flame saying: "Out of the ashes I name thee [quality you wish the subject to learn]." Plant the bulb in the compost, adding the ashes to the compost when cooled.

5 Give the plant to be tended to the one who requested your spell.

Raising energy for spell-work

There are a number of ways to raise energy during spell-work, depending on whether one works alone or with others, one's mobility, the type of spell or simply the preferences of the person putting the spell together. The energy you put into a spell actually begins in the planning stages, at the very start when you are questioning the supplicant—or yourself—to find out what is really needed. There is also the energy of the concentration we lend to a spell while we are

gathering and preparing ingredients, and during the course of the spell as we imbue a symbol with our intent by our focused attention. However, there are specific activities employed expressly within circle-work to raise the energy in order to send a spell out into the ether.

While visualization and concentration produce their own energy forms, they are more generally applied in spell-work to focus on and imbue with our intent the symbols we use to represent what we wish to happen. The same can be said for the activities we engage in to bring the ingredients and form of the spell together prior to casting it. However, there are other kinetic, physical means by which we work to raise energy, including chanting and voice-work, anointing, drumming, dancing and lovemaking. There is more on sex magic on pages 274–275, which will explain the circumstances under which this method of raising energy is used and dispel some of the myths surrounding it.

The theory behind the physical means of raising energy is very simple—all existence in the Universe can be expressed as energy and movement produces and releases energy. Kinetic means of raising and releasing energy in a magically controlled environment serves to empower the spell and to propel it outwards onto the web. In groups, dance and chant serve to bond people to the purpose of the spell-work and act as a way of blending the energies of the participants. It opens the doorway to the deeper self, so that we can communicate outside of spoken or written language and move beyond the symbolic. This provides us with the means to move into an altered state, which better enables us to walk between the worlds.

*Raising energy to empower a spell is
basic to all spell-work.*

Preparation through chakra work

Within our bodies are certain energy points. This has been common knowledge in different parts of the world for millennia, and some healing systems are based on the intricate knowledge of the way these energy points are joined together. In magical work, we open certain energy points in order to become more aware of the natural threads of the great web that are within and around us, and to enable us to conduct that energy to where it may do good. In the West, we have always been aware that we can hold, focus and direct energy through certain energy points on our bodies, even if we have not had a name for them. Since the increased interest in yoga and in Eastern religions, we have become familiar with the term *chakra*, and this is how we now describe these seven energy points.

Guidelines for opening the chakras are found on page 139 in the advice pertaining to preparation for visualization. This preparation is exactly the same for spell-work and ritual-work as it is for visualization; it involves us consciously enlivening and opening those energy points that help us direct and be a conduit for the energies within and around us. If you work with a group you may find that more experienced members have a moment's silence and concentration, and arrive at preparation much more quickly than is implied in these instructions. With practice and repetition the energy points are quicker to respond, and it is possible to enter very quickly into an altered state of consciousness.

Some groups prefer to run through the exercise of opening chakras or tapping into Earth/Sky energy and linking it in a loop through the body by having one member guide the whole group through the process. This works equally well. When some members become very experienced and sensitive to changes in energy levels, it is possible to reduce the time spent on this exercise because members will attain a suitably prepared level of consciousness in a very short time. There is no particular virtue in speed—and if you need to take your time this does not make you less powerful or an inferior witch—the point is to reach an appropriate state of preparedness, not run a race!

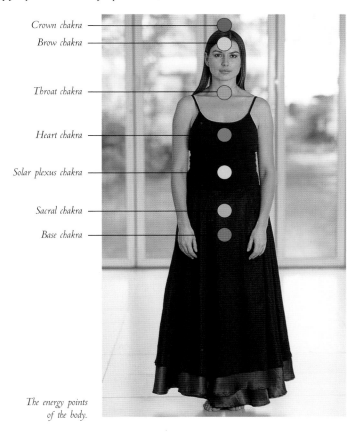

Crown chakra

Brow chakra

Throat chakra

Heart chakra

Solar plexus chakra

Sacral chakra

Base chakra

The energy points of the body.

Chanting to raise energy

Chanting is a traditional way of raising power.

Chanting is a good way to raise the type of energy needed to empower and send out a spell. The repetition, combined with the sounds produced, can be soporific, lulling the active, thinking mind into a state of momentary suspension, while the mysterious creative, right-brain functions, which many magicians suspect is linked with psychic abilities, can come out to play. I have certainly experienced the lulling effect, but cannot speak for which brain cells, if any, kicked into action as a result.

Different from chanting, voice-work, which aims to produce prolonged notes of specific frequency, teaches us that frequency can key into particular energies, which can be called into the circle and sent out again. There is a psychological and cultural element to this; minor keys, for example, are culturally linked with melancholy, mystery and the past and so may access energies within us that correlate with such associations. Elements of this are present in chant and, in combination with the principle of repetition and altered consciousness, this makes chant a particularly powerful tool.

Another function of chant is to help us focus; it helps if the chant is suitable for the proceedings. A good example of this would be using an upbeat, fast-tempo chant, the words of which relate to the element of Air for a communications spell. "With my feathers I fly/As an arrow I fly/Straight to the arms of the Goddess I fly." When working on a spell to bring about a transformation in your life, you might use the old Wiccan favorite: "She changes everything She touches/And everything She touches changes." There are many standards that are used in the pagan community, and you will hear many of these at campfires and at circles. However, some wonderful chants are available on CD and tape and over the internet on alternative and world music sites.

While chanting solo or with others can be a powerful way of raising energy, it can be wonderful combined with simple drumming patterns. However, if you use this method, you will need to ensure that the drumming does not drown out the voice. The drummer will need to be sensitive to the primacy of the chant.

Drumming, dance and visualization

Most methods of raising energy also serve to help participants make the transition from everyday consciousness to between-the-worlds consciousness. Drumming is an excellent example of this, and is often the chosen method for those who wish to enter into spiritual and developmental work in a drastically altered level of consciousness. There are theories about the links between the drum and our heartbeats, and psychology and musicology experiments have been carried out to map these connections. It seems that if we allow ourselves to enter the drumbeat and concentrate on the rhythms, in some circumstances our own pulses alter to match it.

Drumming aids a shift in consciousness to enable spell-work.

In circle-work, the link between drumbeat and pulse is used in much the same way as chant is deployed: to distract the left-hand brain functions; to tap into those psychological, physiological and cultural associations that are helpful in altering our state of consciousness; and to raise energy by calling it in and sending it out. Traditionally, drumming is for calling in, whether we are invoking an element, a deity or specific forms of energy. I have been to several festivals where drumming has been blamed for the torrential rains that seem to come out of nowhere to spoil an otherwise sunny day! However, I have also observed that drumming is good for "sending" energy, too.

There are several different patterns of beat that help to raise energy and alter consciousness in a circle: Waltz timing is popular because the three beats are associated with the triple Goddess; other rhythms seem to work just as well. Simplicity is of the essence, particularly if drumming is going to be combined with chants. Again, the best way to experience this is working in a circle where drumming is used or around a campfire. In addition, there are good DVDs, CDs and tapes of drumbeats used in Wicca, all available on alternative and world music internet sites.

The last form of raising energy for spell-work and ritual is dance—most often in covens this refers to simple rhythmic movement rather than complicated dancesteps. It is best for circles where people have full mobility, though I have participated in some pretty nifty formation wheelchair dances in the circle! The same principles apply as with chanting and drumming; dance is perhaps the most fully physical of these, and can be combined very effectively with both.

Kinetic movement such as dance is good for empowering ritual and spell-work.

Sex magic

Until relatively recently, it has been difficult to speak publicly about sex in a ritual context because of the sensationalist media inventions of orgies and the rather more damaging slanders concerning the abuse of minors. The care and protection of children is seen as a sacred undertaking in Wicca, so the wild and unfounded accusations against the community linked to allegations of so-called Satanic Abuse in the 1980s particularly rankled. After the FBI and investigating commissions in other countries publicly concluded that fundamentalist Christian groups had deliberately orchestrated this blood libel, many witches chose to distance themselves publicly from any connection between ritual and sex. This is understandable as many Wiccan parents were concerned about the implications of social services taking an over-zealous interest in their child-raising abilities.

However, we are now moving into an era of greater tolerance and more public awareness of Wicca as a spiritual path as it comes of age. Just as Wicca has come to maturity, it follows that we should deal with sex in an adult manner. Needless to say, when I speak of sex and sexuality I am referring only to consenting adults; when I speak of sexual orientation I am speaking of being heterosexual, gay or bisexual and some of the delicate nuances that dance between these definitions. Pedophilia—sexual interest in children—is not a sexual orientation; it is a dysfunction and if enacted is an act of violence.

Sexual energy is primal energy; it is a sacred form of energy which cultures believe brings humans closer to the divine. Between two freely consenting people, usually a committed couple who work together, sex in the circle raises energy that can be directed toward magical work. Provided that the act itself is in keeping with the rule "harm none," it is as valid a method for engendering energy and sending it out as chanting, drumming or dance.

A controversy that has rumbled on for many years within the Craft is the issue of sexual polarity. More accurately gender polarity, this principle is based on the assertion that all acts of magic must comprise a correct balance of masculine and feminine in order to make magic. This is unfounded: gay men, lesbians and bisexual men and women, men working together and women working together can empower a spell as effectively as a heterosexual male and female working together. If there is male and female in nature, there is also hermaphroditism and homosexuality.

Sex magic should be consensual and should be conducted with respect.

Directing and releasing energy

Directing and releasing energy takes place at various points in circle-work. Although part of the function of the circle's boundary is to contain energy until it is ready for release, this does not mean that it is raised throughout the circle only to be released when the circle is opened again. There are several points at which directing and releasing takes place.

The most obvious example of directing energy occurs when casting the circle in the first place. In this case, you draw energy through your body and direct it through the solar plexus, down the arms and through the athame blade, wand or finger to form a circle of energy. This is not, strictly speaking, a release of energy since the circle stays in place until it gently disperses and joins the Earth again or is drawn back through the person who originally cast it.

In a group there is sometimes a point when energy is released into the ether to go and do its work. An example of this can be found in healing work, where a circle of people holding hands first direct the

energy they are about to raise to a named person or persons. They say the name aloud, then visualize that person well and happy. The group raises energy by moving deosil in a dance, perhaps chanting. If a group is experienced in working together, there will be a point when everyone recognizes spontaneously that the energy has reached its optimum point. Some groups nominate a person to facilitate and judge when the energy is high enough and this person will signal when to release. Either way, when the time is ripe everyone raises their arms, hands still joined, and releases the energy skyward—sometimes with a shout or the last word of the chant to send it on its way. This does not break the circle, but it does release the energy raised for spell-work.

The two tools used most to direct energy in this way are the athame and the wand. The athame is most commonly used to cast circles, describe pentagrams and to direct energy when symbols are being named as that which they represent. Wands can be used to cast circles, but are also commonly deployed when the element of Air is invoked to carry the spell swiftly onwards.

Many witches use an athame or wand with which to direct energy raised for circle-casting.

developing
skills and
knowledge

Developing your magical powers

W icca is a path of learning; much of it experiential, some derived from research and study. Experience is most important, but acquiring basic information has its place.

There is a great difference, though, between information and practice, and the difference is knowledge. Knowledge is the deeper sense of realization that comes from direct experience of a truth. In Wicca, we can know what is true, but can only experience a truth for ourselves.

This is also true of *the mysteries*, a term you may come across in references to the Craft. Many people come to Wicca believing that because it is sometimes termed a mystery religion, certain secret information will be passed to them as they progress. The simple fact is that no one can teach or tell you the mysteries as these are realizations that reveal themselves as a result of your own spiritual experiences, through circle-work and direct contact with nature. You may find, when you try to share that knowledge, that you have trouble putting it into words, or that the

Learning about magic involves gaining new skills and developing your knowledge.

realization is so profound that it sounds simple and unimpressive when you try to express it. And perhaps that is as it should be.

You can develop your intuitive powers through visualization, dream-work and circle-work. It takes practice and sometimes comes in unexpected ways. Developing "psychic" powers is not so much about predicting the winning numbers in the lottery as it is about enhancing your sensitivity toward random thoughts and learning how to decipher emotional changes within yourself. It may be as simple as having a sense of when the phone will ring or spotting coincidences and working out whether synchronicity is random or sometimes carries a particular meaning for you. This is part of being a patterner and a weaver of magic.

This section offers you a range of exercises to help you develop your abilities. It includes useful glossaries, outlines of Wiccan traditions and basic information on other relevant sources and methods of spiritual and magical growth. It is a good idea to start your own Book of Shadows now if you are working your way through this book gradually. This record of your own magical and spiritual development is a place to keep favorite magical recipes and results and can be added to as you progress in the Craft.

Meditation

Meditation is not all about transcendentalism or rising above the physical or daily reality of our existence—the separation of spirit and body is not an aspiration within Wiccan religion and practice. Meditation can take place in many different situations; some may include rhythmic movement such as dancing, digging a garden, knitting, spinning or weaving. Other stiller forms of meditation may include a focus of concentration such as gazing into a candleflame. As one old hand once remarked to me after hearing a talk on chakra work and meditation: "Meditation, eh? We used to call it looking into the fire."

The objectives of meditation may differ; sometimes it is possible to meditate on a particular issue or symbol or question while carrying out repetitive physical activities. At other times it may be possible to practice being with a particular emotion or state of consciousness, initially by concentrating on an object or movement in the outside world, until we are still enough to be able to observe certain truths about ourselves and our dealings in the world.

Attaining a sense of stillness makes us more aware of energy changes within and around us.

Practicing different forms of meditation will enhance and develop your skills in circle-work as well as your spiritual and magical development. Although one would hesitate to use the word *discipline*, practicing the alteration of one's state of consciousness on a regular basis makes us more aware of those changes in energy that one encounters in the circle. See if you can perform a "moving meditation" through rhythmic movement or when performing a repetitive task; is it easy to let your mind slip away from your surroundings? Or try focusing on an object and slow your breathing in order to enter a daydream state of consciousness. Only experimentation will reveal what works for you.

Regular meditation also helps to enliven the spark of magic within by building our trust and understanding of our own intuitive powers. It also helps us build our inner strength as human beings, to discover our inner resources, our integrity and our beauty.

Regular meditation can help to broaden our spiritual and psychological vision.

Dreams and dream-work

Dreaming is such a mysterious activity that in spite of extensive scientific research, there is still no single theory on its purpose and function. Psychologists argue that dreams are symbolic of our inner desires. However, other evidence suggests that dreams help regulate our emotions, manage, and consolidate our memories, help us learn new mental skills and work through the tensions and stresses of the day. Dreaming also has spiritual significance.

Some cultures maintain that while a person is dreaming, their spirit leaves their body and meets with others, either in the Spirit world where we also encounter the dead, or on an astral plane which only the dreaming mind or spirit beings can access. Other cultures believe that the spirit roams the physical world of our consensual reality.

There are various beliefs about the purpose and function of dreaming within Wicca, but many of us do take careful note of our dreams. Physiologically speaking, the emotional centers of the brain are engaged and active when we dream, and given that intuition and emotions are doorways through which we access our magical abilities and deeper selves, it makes sense to listen to what dreams have to tell us. Dreams, like spell-work, often operate in symbolic terms. However, it is only possible to decide whether dreaming about a pink elephant playing a trombone is deeply significant or the result of too much cheese before bedtime if we keep note of our dreams on a regular basis. Very often, it is our discernment of the patterns of the messages sent from self to self, rather than singular symbols, that aid our comprehension.

The best way of tracking patterns is to keep a dream diary. Keep a notebook and pen by your bed to record key aspects of a dream whenever you wake up— whether during the night or first thing in the morning. Writing at least three words to remind you of a dream whenever you wake can be an interesting exercise in itself; the brain tends not to waste much memory on dreams and we forget about them quickly. Keep a pad and pen by your bed for a week and train yourself to write down three important words as an aide-mémoire that will help your recall. I have awoken from what I assumed to be unbroken sleep only to find words written in my dream diary that immediately recall a rich and involved dream I had during the night— and which I would not have remembered had it not been for this nocturnal intervention. Try this method to aid your recall.

Witches know that it is wise to take note of what our dreams have to tell us.

It is important to note the phases of the Moon alongside your dreams. Most witches find that as we connect with the natural rhythms around us, certain aspects of nature's cycles drive our own, inner rhythms. Nowhere is this more obvious than in our dreams. Women may find that their cycle of ovulation and bleeding impacts upon the types of dreams that they have. Some men have reported finding themselves similarly affected by a female partner's cycle and that their dreams, too, tend to work to a similar rhythm. It helps to know what your individual pattern is; for example, I noticed very early on that my deepest and most profound insights into magic and spirituality come at Dark Moon, so I tend to trust that the messages from these dreams are genuine signals from deeper self rather than the result of late-night indigestion. Some people may find that at Full Moon, their dreams are wild, even scrambled, whereas others will have their most significant spiritual moments in dreams at that phase.

Keeping a record is the best way to identify patterns in our dreams.

The notion of dream symbolism has spawned an entire industry in dream interpretation; often dream dictionaries claim to be able to define and interpret universal meanings to particular symbols. However, these tend not to take into account specific cultural and social differences or individual experience and mindsets. Culturally, symbolism differs considerably between cultures; a white flower in England means purity while in Japan it signifies death. We do not exist separately from these cultural meanings and they are bound to impact on us at a deep level. Socially, individuals psychologically assign meanings to particular signals: scent, objects, colors and so forth. While some people have the gift of insight into other people's dreams, there are no hard and fast truths concerning all dreams or all dreamers. We have to construct our own dream dictionaries by observing the significance of our personal iconography, and in turn we can learn a great deal about ourselves.

You may have had the experience of being conscious, while dreaming, that you are in fact dreaming. This is known as lucid dreaming and in the craft we use this form of consciousness to do useful exploratory work. When we become adept at entering and prolonging this state, we may even use it for ritual work. This method of spell-working can have some powerful results. It has the advantage of allowing your imagination to manifest in ways that are more immediate; for example, invoking the elements or deities in a dream can result in a visual manifestation not usually experienced in circle-work. This is turn can make it easier for us to focus on the objectives of a spell and direct our energies toward achieving them.

If you do experience lucid dreams, it offers a unique opportunity to explore your own, inner landscape. You will visit there in visualization work, and even consciously build aspects of it in some visualization exercises, but dream-time offers you a chance to view the unconscious worlds from the viewpoint of an insider/outsider—a dreamer who is conscious—and offers yet another way of walking between the worlds. I take careful note of my encounters with figures

I meet in dreamtime, as I have found that these are often manifestations of the Goddess within.

Dreams can offer spiritual revelations as well as insights into everyday problems. But they do more than reveal truths; they can also offer guidance on how to put this knowledge into action. The wisdom of dreams is not to be found in dream dictionaries, but in our developed understanding of their meaning to us as individuals.

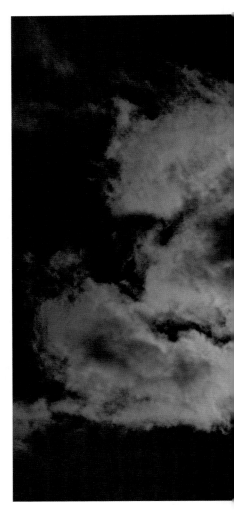

Dreams are often spiritual revelations.

Astrology

There are many debates about the validity of astrology as a means of deciphering the character and fate of an individual. Just as some dream dictionaries claim to link universal meanings to individual symbol systems, some astrologers claim to be able to map the traits and future of individuals without taking into account their complex social and cultural backgrounds and experiences. The truth may be somewhere in between. While it makes sense for people born at a certain time of year to share some traits, one also witnesses the fact that a Leo born into a wealthy family has a number of advantages that leads them on to a different path from a counterpart born on the same day into a working-class family.

In Wiccan terms, the 12-sign zodiac so familiar in the West is regarded as a useful symbolic system. What we call our star-sign is more accurately our Sun sign—the sign that the Sun was in when we were born. This little nascent signature was joined, in medieval times, with one's rising and Moon signs. The rising sign is the constellation coming over the eastern horizon at the exact time of your birth and the Moon sign is the constellation through which the Moon was traveling at that time. Put at its simplest, the Sun sign indicates one's true nature, the Moon sign denotes emotional traits, while the rising sign is the mask or public face we show to the world. Given the number of permutations possible between triple combinations of 12 Sun-signs, 12 Moon-signs and 12 Ascendants,

Our so-called "star" signs are actually our solar signs.

this provides a far more individually adjustable insight. This triangulated method gave our ancestors a slightly more refined means by which to judge the character traits and fortune of an individual.

Imagine then, the fine nuances of interpretation possible when an individually drawn nascent chart is divided into various astrological houses, ruling different aspects of life, and the position of all the planets is observed in relation to each other and the moment of one's birth. Many working groups like to have an astrologer provide charts for its members. This is because the different signs are related to different elements, and some people feel that this is a useful guide to the likely energy balance of a group. It doesn't matter that some groups may find that they are mostly Air or Fire signs—but knowing the starting point of the group's balance may sometimes explain group dynamics and enable a group to use this understanding in order to work to their strengths.

Astrology is often used in the timing of spell-work.

Astrology is sometimes used in the timing of magical work (see pages 206–209); since the Moon is so important in magical work, some witches like to use the path of the Moon in relation to the constellations in order to maximize their chances of success in spell-work. However, there is more to astrology than nascent charts and star-signs; this is just one way of interpreting the influence of the planets. In magic, we often use the symbolism of the planets to empower our spells, calling upon their influence in much the same way that we call upon the elements or the deities.

In terms of planetary symbolism, we tend to refer to the following planets in our solar system; Mercury, Venus, Mars, Jupiter, Saturn, Pluto, Uranus and Neptune, with an emphasis on the first five. In addition, we use the Moon, though strictly speaking our nearest celestial neighbor is a satellite and not a planet, and the Sun, which is not a planet but a star.

Tarot

Though the origins of the Tarot remain elusive, we do know that decks of Tarot cards started appearing in the noble courts of Italy in the fourteenth century. Mythology regarding their development includes the claim that Tarot originated in ancient Egypt, but there is little evidence for this. Today it is most commonly used as a tool for divination, though in Wicca the symbols of the Tarot deck are also used in meditation and spell-work.

A Tarot deck consists of 72 cards, all of which symbolize arcane aspects of events, character and influences in our lives. There are 22 major arcana—cards that depict objects and/or figures symbolizing major life influences and/or events. There are also four suits of cards: Cups, coins, blades and rods, numbering one to ten per suit, known as "pip" cards; and four ruling court cards, King, Queen, Knight and Page, attached to each suit. In modern decks the nomenclature of the major arcana and court cards may vary.

The origins of the Tarot are elusive, but date back hundreds of years.

The four suits correspond with the first four sacred elements in Wicca—cups with Water, coins with Earth, blades with Air and rods with Fire. In most Wiccan circles, the symbolism for Air and Fire is reversed. This makes it easy for witches to assimilate the classification of the suits in the Tarot. The same is true of the major arcana, which equate in different ways to Wiccan esoteric symbolism and encapsulate at a simple yet profound level the physical, psychological and spiritual aspects of the human condition.

In divination, the cards have positive and negative connotations according to the aspect they form with neighboring cards in a spread. The combination of the symbols and the positions of the cards provide for an amazingly subtle reading, as the permutations are almost endless. However, at the level of the cards themselves, there are a number of other nuances of meaning; for example the elemental and sub-elemental significance of the court cards, which throws further possibilities into the mix. This is why the Tarot is a lifetime study. For more in-depth study you will need to seek out classes or workshops run by experienced readers and refer to standard works on Tarot.

The suits: pip cards

Suit	Element	Attributes
Coins	Earth	Wealth, physical health, material matters
Cups	Water	Emotions, love and relationships
Rods	Fire	Energy, activity, projects
Blades	Air	The mind, legal matters, communication, conflict

The functions and meanings of the cards as outlined below incorporate both positive and negative facets of the cards, and are extremely basic in their guidance. The court cards have their own sub-elemental significance, regardless of the suit with which they are associated. For example, the King card is associated with Fire. In the suit of blades—Air—this card becomes the "Fire of Air." This means that this card is the acting aspect of Air—one who influences communication, intellect or conflict. The court cards always represent actual people if you are reading for divination purposes.

A court card and a pip card from a popular Tarot deck.

Che numbers and courc cards

I	Foundation	8	Arrival
2	Others	9	Obstacles
3	Society, aid, influences	10	Completion
4	Consolidation	King	Fire
5	Transition	Queen	Water
6	Movement	Knight	Air
7	Building or destroying	Page	Earth

The major arcana

0 The Fool	Beginnings, trust, foolishness, sagacity
1 Magus	Raw energy, preparation
2 High Priestess	Intuition, secret knowledge
3 Empress	Fertility, creativity, material matters, nurture
4 Emperor	Worldly power, responsibilities, command, oppression
5 Heirophant	Knowledge and wisdom, restriction, convention
6 Lovers	Relationships, passion, binding, obsession
7 Chariot	Movement, progression, delay, limitations
8 Strength	Control over the material, spiritual and physical alignment
9 Hermit	Enlightenment, wisdom, isolation
10 Wheel of Fortune	Cycles, rises and falls in status/wealth
11 Justice	Balance, cause and effect, righting wrongs
12 Hanged Man	Labor for gain, patience, suspension, stalemate
13 Death	Transformation, life cycles, resignation
14 Temperance	Life balance, thresholds, health, lifestyle, adjustment
15 Devil	Misconception, physicality, waste
16 Tower	Upheaval, disruption, irrevocable change, breakthrough
17 Star	Opportunities, lucky meetings, sharing wisdom
18 Moon	Intuition, female cycles, mental health issues, illusion
19 Sun	Health, success, happiness, generosity
20 Judgement	Understanding, resurrection, revival, bigotry, prejudice
21 World	Attainment, achievement, fulfilment

DIVINATION SPREADS

There are a number of standard divination spreads, for which guidance can be found in good Tarot books and on the Web. The best known is the Celtic Cross spread—an arrangement of ten cards, chosen at random and laid out and read in the following order with the labeled meanings ascribed to the card that turns up in that respective position. Another spread popular with Wiccans is the three-card spread for a direct answer to a specific problem or situation—three cards are chosen from the major arcana by the questioner and laid as below:

Celtic Cross spread

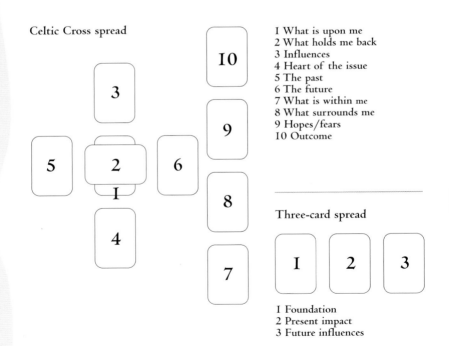

1 What is upon me
2 What holds me back
3 Influences
4 Heart of the issue
5 The past
6 The future
7 What is within me
8 What surrounds me
9 Hopes/fears
10 Outcome

Three-card spread

1 Foundation
2 Present impact
3 Future influences

Traditionally, a Tarot reader should be given her/his first set of cards, but many prefer to choose their own. Some people like to keep their cards wrapped in a black silk cloth or pouch and prohibit others, apart from questioners, from touching them. Witches tend to consecrate their decks in a circle, blessing the deck with purification incense (see page 342) before use.

MEDITATION

Witches also use Tarot cards for meditation. The 22 major arcana cards are a sequence of images, representing a cycle of the material, psychological and spiritually integrated progression of an individual. Given their significance, the major arcana provides opportunities for psychic storytelling and as a tool of focus for meditation. A good example of this would be the case of someone seeking to reconcile spirituality with the material and finding their own, innate median in this balance; an ideal card to focus on would be the Strength card. This card can be placed on an altar for in-circle meditation, or by the bedside as the first and last thing a person sees.

SPELL-WORK

The symbolism of the Tarot is particularly useful to witches in spell-work. When working a binding or banishing spell, for example, it is useful to have the Hermit card, which is associated with restrictive and disciplinarian Saturn, on the altar. This helps the spell-caster to focus on the particular form of energy they are summoning to witness and aid them in their endeavor. The power of a healing spell may be enhanced if the magician has the Temperance card present to help them concentrate on the nature of the work they are carrying out. Similarly, magical work for career success for a friend is benefited by the presence of the Star card, which symbolizes luck in opportunities arising.

Scrying

Scrying—which means "to discern"—is the technique of focusing on a magical tool such as a mirror, a crystal ball or a flame in order to receive images and thoughts that reveal a truth or a message concerning a particular situation. In order to discern the meaning of these, it is necessary to find the patterns present in whatever it is we have perceived—and we witches are great patterners.

The popular perception of scrying is that gazing into a magical crystal ball enables the reader to physically see the future, rather like watching a video. Actually, there are very few people who experience this; the gift is peculiar to them and not the crystal ball. What actually happens when scrying differs between individuals. The theory about scrying is similar to that of chanting or dancing when preparing for magical or vision work. The craft occupies or distracts the left-hand side of the brain (which operates our thinking and rational faculties) in order that the right-hand side of the brain (equated with the random, the creative, the chaotic) is released from the

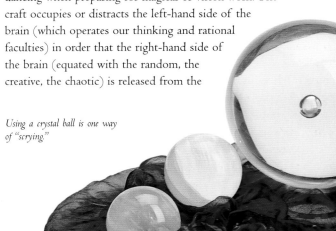

Using a crystal ball is one way of "scrying."

298

policing of the left side, enabling it to give rein to its psychic aspects. There is a paradox present here—we have to focus and concentrate in order to enable part of our minds to drift.

The art of scrying swings into gear when we try to capture the fleeting thoughts and images, and piece them

Mirrors are popular means of divination.

together to make some sense. This is not always easy, as it involves having to deliberately set aside what we know in order to acknowledge what we see. Since none of us are value- or bias-free in our judgements, this can be a tall order! However, the more we practice our visionary abilities, the stronger they impress themselves upon us, and this, along with experience and the testing of actual outcomes against our insights, makes interpretation become easier as time goes by.

The means by which we choose to scry in the Wiccan community and the traditions we associate with each method differ considerably. The very practical among us suspect that a good scryer can get as valid a result from observing the pattern on a paisley rug as they can from an expensive and rare crystal ball.

One of the most popular means of scrying in the Wiccan community is via the ubiquitous crystal ball. The most common is clear quartz crystal, tumbled and polished to a perfect sphere. The faults in quartz answer all the specifications for a natural scrying tool. The effects produced by flaws such as prismic refraction can serve to draw the scryer into the stone very quickly and effectively. Some witches prefer more opaque stone such as smoky quartz or amethyst. Others plump for pink rose quartz. Although black obsidian spheres look incredibly dramatic, they are not as helpfully distracting as flawed crystal.

The use of reflective surfaces in scrying betrays its ancient antecedents; the most perfect "mirror" for this purpose is a lake of clear water under the stars. Of course, if you don't happen to have one in your backyard, you could do worse than to employ a bowl of clean water under a starry sky or in a room filled with candlelight. Water is a powerfully psychic element and its close proximity during scrying tends to magnify our intuitive faculties. It is best to use a plain silver or black bowl in order to produce a sense of depth. In water- or mirror-scrying (a black or darkened mirror is a fair second to a bowl of water), the trick is to look into its depths. Starlight or candlelight can produce interesting patterns to keep your consciousness occupied while images, words or thoughts flow in.

Flame-gazing is a favorite occupation in my own household—it was the existence of an open fireplace that clinched the deal when I bought my present home. As well as providing a great place to dry out herbs naturally, and a natural focus for spell-work, a lit fire can be an excellent focal point for scrying. There is something extremely primal about the energy of fire from wood or other natural materials, and the very human attraction to the fireside that makes scrying in the flames arguably the easiest of scrying techniques. An open fire has the double advantage of providing visible occupation for the left brain as well as providing pictures for the right brain to capture.

Whatever method of scrying you come to favor, it is important to realize that there is no set way of doing it successfully—only hints, tips and guidelines. With perseverance, you will find your own talent and identify your own preferred method for scrying.

Candles and open fires are excellent
for flame-gazing.

The Qabalah

The Qabalah, sometimes known as the "Tree of Life," is a magical map, a bit like the system of the Tarot in conception. Derived from ancient Jewish mysticism, it consists of Sephira or spheres, with pathways between. The Sephira are aspects of life and spiritual enlightenment, and each has planetary and angelic correspondences. Some intrepid mappers have even managed to map the Tarot directly onto the paths between the Sephira.

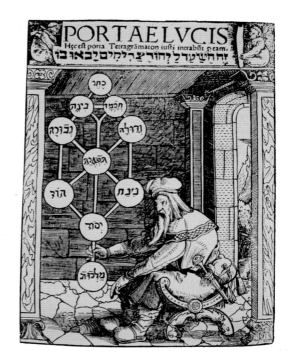

The term qabalah *means "received tradition."*

The Craft is an eclectic path and consequently witches tend to be inclusive and inquisitive in their practices. We incorporate those tools, techniques, traditions and systems we find relevant, and honor those ancestors whose endeavors produced the means by which we can work to attain knowledge. We also acknowledge that the origin of some of these systems was a very different time, place and culture from our present one, and if we tear some techniques or ideas away from their moorings, we had better be clear what we are doing!

The Qabalah is just such a system. Many esoteric and mystery traditions of the West (for example, the Golden Dawn and the Rosicrucians) were heavily influenced by Qabalistic tradition. Aleister Crowley, the early twentieth-century bad boy of occult magic, was fascinated with what is known as the "artificial" Qabalah which concentrates on abstruse notions of numerology and angelic forms. The system with which most Wiccans are familiar is the natural Qabalah, a system of ten Sephiroth with 22 pathways connecting them.

Tradition has it that the Qabalah was originally given to Moses on Mount Sinai by JHWH—the god of the Jews—and handed down by oral tradition. The word QBLH actually means "received tradition" but is sometimes used synonymously with the term "hidden wisdom." The Qabalah is a body of occult knowledge which is supposed to contain the secrets of the Universe, thought variously to be arrived at through direct experience of the Sephiroth and the pathways between, or through the underlying principles that could be derived through logical numeric systems. It is also sometimes referred to as a map of consciousness, indicating the variety of interpretations to which it is subject.

Perhaps the easiest way to understand its multiple nature and purpose is to see the ten Sephiroth as forming the basis of the manifestation of the Universe, the nature of the divine and a path by which a human being can become divine and unite with the Godhead.

The Sephiroth, when arranged in the Tree of Life (see pages 308–309), provide a structure via which the mysteries of the Qabalah can be studied and experienced. Arranged in a geometric pattern, the Sephira are linked by 22 paths. Although these paths were originally representative of the Hebrew alphabet and the energies associated with the power of each individual letter, nowadays witches tend to associate them more closely with the 22 major arcana of the Tarot. There are a number of overlays provided by modern innovative mapping—including an association with the Nordic runes and one with the Celtic Tree Alphabet (see pages 346–347)—indicating the enduring power and appeal of the original symbolism and structure of the Sephiroth.

The ten Sephiroth and the interlinking pathways are laid out (right) in order to better demonstrate the geometric patterns, connections and color symbolism of the system. In Wicca, each sphere relates to a planetary correspondence, as well as an aspect of the material,

the sephiroth

The ten Sephiroth carry the following meanings:

Sephiroth	Attribute
Kether	Crown
Chokmah	Wisdom
Binah	Understanding
Chesed	Mercy
Geburah	Strength
Tiphareth	Splendor/beauty
Netzach	Victory
Hod	Glory
Yesod	Foundation
Malkuth	Kingdom

Characteristics	Color	Cosmic Association/Planet
Union with the divine, spiritual attainment	White	The Spiral/Neptune
Energy in motion, Father	Grey	The Zodiac/Uranus (God-force)
Keeping silence, protective strength, Mother	Black	Saturn (Goddess-force)
Gain, opportunity, building, justice, plenty, knowledge of inner self	Blue	Jupiter
Courage, dispersement, change, critical faculties	Red	Mars
Healing, harmony, teaching, success	Yellow	Sun
Sexuality, relationships, giving, love, art	Green	Venus
Communication, truthfulness, revelation, magic	Orange	Mercury
Intuition, psychic powers, mental health, emotions, dreams	Violet	Moon
Physicality, home, guidance, material growth	Multi-colored	Earth

psychological and spiritual development of the self. Witches who are particularly interested in ceremonial or esoteric magical systems take an interest in the angelic forms associated with each sphere, but generally recourse to angelic forms is a matter for individuals. In addition to the ten main Sephiroth there is the domain of Daath (Day-arth) or Knowledge, known as the Abyss. This lies in the Tree of Life between Binah, Chokmah, Geburah and Chesed and directly on the path between Tiphareth and Kether.

In many covens, basic training prior to initiation includes guided visualizations based on the ten Sephiroth; these are more accurately designated *path-working* though this term is used interchangeably with *guided visualization*. An experienced coven member is made responsible for facilitating inner journeys to spheres on the Tree of Life via one of the 22 pathways that link them together.

An early journey in this type of training takes the acolyte to the Sephira of Yesod, and many would-be initiates are delighted by what they find in the Temple of the Moon. The path of the Tree of Life, however, is fraught with dangers, and it is common for newcomers to Qabalah to become so entranced by their early discoveries in Yesod that they can become stuck there and find difficulty in moving on. Interestingly, one of the negative aspects of the Moon card in the Tarot is that of illusion—and one who is "moonstruck" can become obsessed with their own powers and mistake illusion for reality. This is an early lesson in the power of the Qabalah—accessing this system of discovery should never be undertaken lightly and it is a good idea to have experienced company on the path.

The best way for a beginner to approach the Tree of Life is to do so in acknowledgement that this is a pared down, concentrated and potent expression of a whole body of philosophy with ancient and mystical origins. What you find on the pathways within the Sephiroth may be peculiar to your own experience but will share common ground with the experiences of others; this is why it is mapped. If you decide to explore the Qabalah alone, it is a good idea to keep a diary to record your experiences on your journey, your dreams and any synchronicity you notice in your everyday life. This will allow you to see if you are becoming stuck or have become distracted and wandered off track altogether, as well as recording your rich and varied explorations of the Tree of Life.

The Qabalah is based on Judaic mystic tradition. Jacob's Ladder, seen here, is another expression of the Tree of Life.

Tree of Life

The Tree of Life is found in various forms in cultures all over the world and is a common expression of the nature of the Universe and of life. The Tree of Life (depicted opposite) is based on the ancient system of the Qabalah, and shows a structure of archetypal spheres organized in a geometric pattern which simplify the complex nature of reality. This "map" has evolved over time and is subject to various interpretations and purposes. Ostensibly providing a map of the Universe that describes and delineates its creation, it is also considered to be a map of the human psyche and a guide to spiritual enlightenment.

If you are putting together your own Book of Shadows, you might consider copying down the basic structure of the Sephiroth as set out here, leaving space for notes to be added as you progress on the path. The Tree of Life is particularly susceptible to overlays of multi- and inter-cultural systems of knowledge, as well as multiple layers of correspondences that link with it. You are likely to want to add your own discoveries and contributions to the sum of your developing knowledge as you go along.

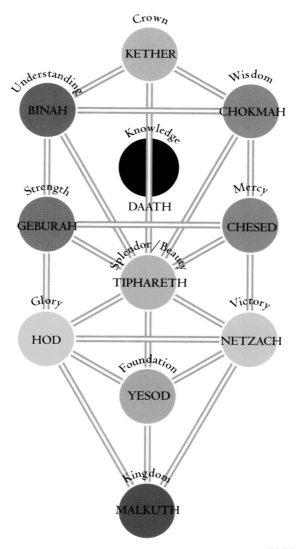

Crown
KETHER

Understanding
BINAH

Wisdom
CHOKMAH

Knowledge
DAATH

Strength
GEBURAH

Mercy
CHESED

Splendor / Beauty
TIPHARETH

Glory
HOD

Victory
NETZACH

Foundation
YESOD

Kingdom
MALKUTH

Alchemy

The word *alchemy* usually conjures up images of medieval labs, replete with mysterious liquids and metals in glass alembics. While part of this image has a basis in fact, the philosophical basis of alchemy is based on an amalgamation of spiritual philosophies and theories. The first known adept of alchemy was Hermes Trismegistus who lived in Egypt almost four thousand years ago. He is credited with writing the *Hermetica*, 42 volumes embodying magical and spiritual philosophies and outlining sacred rituals. Alchemy was practiced in ancient China and in the Far East, and the early Greek philosophers who generated theories about the composition of matter influenced its development, particularly regarding the theory of the elements Air, Fire, Water and Earth. It came to Europe in medieval times via Arabian adepts working in Spain.

Alchemists pursued the chemical code that contained the secrets of the Universe.

The search for the philosopher's stone was nothing more or less than the quest of the soul to reach perfection. While alchemists endeavored to transmute base metals to gold, and find the elusive elixir of life, they were also attempting to duplicate what was thought to be a natural process—the means by which all things strive to reach perfection. In short, although attempting physical changes by chemical means, alchemists were aware that the philosophy on which this was based carried a code that explained our place in the Universe.

Alchemy has been intertwined with magic and astrological theories from the very earliest times. Its spiritual aspects are still valued by occultists in the West. Although in Wicca the struggle for perfection is a little too transcendental for our earthier spirituality, some of its lessons are still relevant. Its theory of matter composed of Air, Fire, Water and Earth (to which was later added Ether—Spirit) comes from the same source on which this division is founded in Wicca. The astrological and planetary correspondences are familiar to Wiccans because these systems come from the same roots; indeed, it is likely that early Wiccan rituals were strongly influenced by alchemical philosophies, which, like the *Hermetica*, held a great fascination for the key players in its development.

SEVEN KEY METALS

The contemporary relevance of alchemy to Wicca is still seen in tables of correspondences. The seven key metals of alchemy—rising from the base to pure and linked with the seven

The spiritual aspects of alchemy are still valued by occultists in the West.

stages of human spiritual development—are linked with the seven planets of our solar system known to the ancient Greeks.

LEAD

Lead, the most base of metals, was used in great quantities in the ancient world because of its low melting point and malleability. These qualities made it suitable for inscriptions and lead tablets, dating from Roman times and impressed with Latin spells, have been found in sacred wells in Britain. Dense and heavy, lead is the metal of slow, ponderous Saturn. In a modern echo of the ancient correspondence, the rings around Saturn can be seen as symbolic of lead's protective qualities.

TIN

Tin is another soft metal, and was considered to be the gift of Jupiter, the ancient Roman ruler of the gods. Tin played its part in the technological development of civilizations as a component of bronze, which was produced by adding tin to copper to produce a hard metal that resisted corrosion.

IRON

Iron, the metal of Mars, came into its own when the ancient world discovered the secret of smelting and turned it into weapons that could defeat those of bronze. It was also used to manufacture farming tools such as ploughshares— another reason perhaps why fierce Mars, the ancient Roman god of war, is also a patron of farming.

COPPER

Copper, metal of lovely Venus, was once exported in great quantities from Cyprus, whence it derives its name. Cyprus was reputed to be the birthplace of Venus, the goddess of love.

MERCURY

Mercury, planet of the messenger god Hermes, is associated with quicksilver (*quick* denoting "alive"), also known as mercury.

SILVER AND GOLD

The first noble metal in this table is silver, linked with the Moon, while the most noble of metals is gold, associated with the Sun, its life-giving properties and the symbol of spiritual attainment. The marriage of Sun and Moon is known as the "Chemical Wedding" and Wiccans who honor both Goddess and God as aspects of the ultimate being perceive this as an expression of the balance needed in order to attain divinity.

Wicca tends to shy away from this type of hierarchical arrangement; we value the material world as being infused with Spirit rather than a graduation from base to pure. However, for Wiccans, alchemy captures the notion of spiritual attainment as coming out of the matter of the Universe; for us the idea that the secrets of the divine Universe are within and around us has a familiar ring.

The alchemical hierarchy of metals carries a specific meaning within Wicca.

Wiccan symbols

Like most religious paths, Wicca has its storehouse of favorite symbols. The attributes of some are multiple and subject to almost endless connotation and overlay. Some basic interpretations are generally agreed, however, and a brief glossary can be found below.

Witches often wear symbols and images on clothing or in jewelry designs. Occasionally, a symbol is carried or worn for a specific purpose, by way of invoking its power for protection or strength, for example. This is most often the case when we use them to decorate our magical tools, especially chalices, athames and wands or staffs. We also make good use of basic signatory symbols in magic and ritual by carving relevant signs into candles, writing them in ink or describing them in the air with our athames. Elemental and planetary symbols help to focus on the energies we invoke, and at the same time encapsulate their concentrated power.

Some symbols have been rediscovered from ancient sources—the spiral and the labyrinth—while those used for centuries for other purposes, such as mazes, have been reclaimed as sacred signs. Sometimes a path born in the West makes extensive use of symbolism that originated in the East; however as Wicca is an eclectic and diverse spirituality, it honors wisdom wherever it is found. Some witches like to keep to the symbols appropriate to their own particular traditions—but there is no orthodoxy dictating that this must be the case, and witches are more than happy to mix and match in the most respectful way.

THE PENTACLE/PENTAGRAM

One of the most commonly sported symbols in Wicca is the five-pointed star, the pentagram. If encircled it is a pentacle and signifies variously the circle of the Earth or the unified nature of the Universe. The five points pertain to the five sacred elements Air, Fire, Water, Earth and Spirit, and in this form it is worn with the point upwards. When a pentacle or pentagram is seen with the point downwards, this is a protective or banishing symbol and is sometimes found over doorways. When worn as a point-down pentagram, this is sometimes the symbol of the second initiation of traditional Wicca.

The direction of the Elements symbolized by the five points varies, but a common one is shown in the diagram on the right.

SYMBOLS OF THE ELEMENTS

The colors for the five elements are Air–yellow, Fire–red, Water–blue, Earth–green, Spirit–purple or white (see chart on page 78 for further information). Occasionally, you may see triangular pendants, pointing downward. This usually denotes the first initiation, Water, and is beloved of goddess-centered witches as it also carries positive connotations of female physicality. The symbol for each element is an equilateral triangle (see below).

Air
point upward,
traversed by a
horizontal line

Fire
point upward

Earth
point downward,
traversed by a
horizontal line

Water
point downward

Spirit
a pentagram
upward pointing

THE SIX-POINTED STAR

Sometimes known as the Star of David and a symbol of the Jewish faith, in Wicca the six-pointed star bears different connotations. It unites the symbols of the four physical elements (see above) and its symmetry visibly demonstrates the Hermetic principle, "As above, So below." In Wicca, therefore, it is a symbol of Hermetic significance, as well as the conjunction of the elements.

WEBS, MAZES, LABYRINTHS AND SPIRALS

The web is a particularly important symbol in contemporary Wicca; it describes the way we conceive of the physical and spiritual Universe and the nature of magic. It symbolizes sacred connection, which we also understand variously as Spirit and/or the God and Goddess. Mazes, beloved in Europe in medieval and Renaissance times, are symbols of the left-brain functions, of rationality and reason. Walking or tracing a labyrinth, on the other hand, engages the right-brain functions, home of intuitive and psychic abilities. A labyrinth depicts the journey from birth, to death and rebirth, and is found on many of the ancient monuments of the world. The spiral has a similar function—unsurprisingly, as the labyrinth is the pathway through a spiral—and likewise denotes the microcosmic and macrocosmic order of the Universe. The spiral, like the web, is a symbol of the element of Spirit.

TRIANGLES, TRISKELES AND CELTIC KNOTS

Triplicity is a favorite configuration in Wicca and resonates with the mathematical and geometric philosophies of the ancient Greeks and with the spiritual symbols used by our Celtic ancestors. The equilateral triangle was a particularly important shape for ancient Greek architects in search of harmonious balance. It was also a symbol sacred to Athena, patron goddess of Athens and deity of wisdom, mathematics, arts and craft.

Triskeles, the three-legged swirls of Celtic art, depict the power of three—Earth, Water and Fire. Symbolically, they are similar to spirals, and because the number three is sacred to the Triple Moon Goddess, signify goddess energy. Celtic design is replete with spiritual symbolism, not least in the complicated knot-work decoration and design. In Wicca, the single unbroken thread from which they are composed signifies the nature of eternity and the Universe, while the shapes depict the complexity and beauty of life.

THE EIGHT-SPOKED WHEEL

The eight-spoked wheel is a symbol of the sacred year, each spoke representing one of the seasonal Sabbats. It sometimes symbolizes the Wheel of Fortuna, goddess of chance and fate in the Roman pantheon.

THE ANKH AND THE EYE OF HORUS

The ankh is an ancient Egyptian symbol associated with Isis, the All-Mother and goddess of magic and healing. The loop is a yonic—female sexual—symbol, while the downward strut is phallic. In conjunction these bring forth life and so the ankh is seen as the key to fertility, rebirth and eternal life. The Eye of Horus, her divine son, is a protection against evil and a symbol of seeing or wisdom. Horus is a god of health and regeneration, and so his symbol carries some significance for contemporary pagans.

THE GREEN MAN

Ancient depictions of the Green Man, a nature spirit replete with leafy features and often with vegetation emerging from his mouth, can be found all over the British Isles. In Wicca he is seen both as an aspect of the god and as a champion of environmentalism.

GODDESS FIGURES

Goddess figures, either great earthy figures such as the Venus of Willendorf or more slender dagger-shaped figures with stump arms, are popular as pendants in the Wiccan community. Many date back to the Stone Age and symbolize all the attributes of a valued female deity.

THE TRIPLE MOON

A Full Moon disc mounted on each side by waxing and waning crescents is a symbol of the Triple Moon goddess, Maiden, Mother and Crone respectively.

THE SOLAR CROSS

Equal-armed crosses pre-date Christianity and, when encircled, symbolize the powers of the Sun.

CORNUCOPIA

The Horn of Plenty is the symbol of the ancient Roman deity Ceres, goddess of fertility and abundance. The wearing of this symbol generally denotes a wish for abundance on the part of the bearer.

Colors

If you are working your way through this book you will already be aware that in Wicca, color matters. Some witches believe that different spiritual vibrations are produced by different colors, a theory that moves beyond symbolism and is not peculiar to Wicca but more New Age in origin. The glossary below restricts itself to the symbolic associations and correspondences of color.

The five sacred elements in Wicca have specific colors assigned to them (see chart on page 78). However, there are other symbolic properties associated with colors. The following guide is not definitive; as your own experience grows, add your own glossary and correspondences to your Book of Shadows.

WHITE

The color of the Moon, white is often used to invoke lunar energy in spell-work. It is also symbolic of purity and light and is often used in conjunction with other colors to denote these as aspects of the work we are undertaking. Blessing rituals generally use white candles. Because white promotes ideas of innocence, it can also be used to connote initiation and pure intentions.

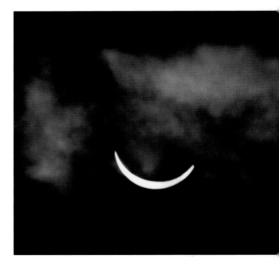

Lunar energy is symbolized by silver or the color white.

BLACK

Contrary to popular belief, black is not a color of evil but the color of potential, of space and protection. It is often used in banishment and binding spells as it is the color denoting the dark part of the Moon as it wanes or the Dark Moon itself.

Black symbolizes darkness; again, in Wicca not conceived of as evil but as potentially creative and inward-reaching. It is a popular color for candles if summoning the dark goddesses such as Hecate, Kali or the Morrigan.

RED

A primary color denoting fire, passion, the will, courage and sexual energy, red is often used in love spells to summon true love. The color of Martian energy, red is used in spell-work to summon defense against that which threatens or oppresses. Red is also used to denote solar energy.

Red can be used to summon Martian energy.

YELLOW

A primary color denoting matters of the mind, communication, learning, movement and beginnings, yellow is the color of goddesses of intellect and study such as Athene and Sarasvarti, and of apprenticeship and studenthood. Like red, it can be used to invoke solar energy, but belongs chiefly to Mercury, planet of swift movement and communication.

Blue is strongly connected with Water associations.

BLUE

A primary color representing Water and consequently healing, harmony, love, emotions, psychic abilities, dreams and intuition, blue is linked with Neptune energy, with darkest blue sometimes symbolizing Jupiter.

GREEN

Green is a symbol of Earth energy.

A secondary color symbolizing fertility, growth, material matters and the Earth, green is also linked with Venus energy. Green is the color of the heart chakra and symbolic of feelings, wholeness and harmonious conjunctions.

PURPLE

In ancient times regarded as the royal color, purple is the color of the planet Jupiter, once seen as king of the gods. Purple denotes spirituality, generosity, justice, serendipity and wonder. Purple is also the color of transformation, which links it back to its association with the element of Spirit. A color linked with Fortuna, goddess of the wheel of fate and chance and with Iris, the messenger goddess of the rainbow (see below).

PINK

This color symbolizes affection, affinity, friendship; pink candles are sometimes used in love spells alongside red and white to add these particular qualities to the others required of a prospective lover.

SILVER

Like white, symbolic of lunar energy, silver is worn by many witches in preference to gold because of the emphasis on Moon phases and other lunar symbolism within Wicca. Silver can also symbolize the need for money in spells for wealth.

GOLD

Gold symbolizes the attributes of the Sun, including happiness, health, fulfilment, success and, according to alchemy, spiritual attainment. Gold is often used in spells to bring health to an individual or general success to an enterprise.

RAINBOW

Strictly speaking, not one color but multi-colored, the rainbow has been adopted as a symbol of gay pride in the West, and Iris, goddess of the rainbow, is its patron. In Wicca the rainbow symbolizes hope, the close interconnection between sky and earth, spirituality and physicality, and the principles of connection, coalition and unity.

herbal lore

Given the time-honored association between witches and herbal knowledge, it is unsurprising that contemporary Wiccans draw on the traditions of magical herbalism. Just as there are symbolic correspondences between planets, constellations, Moon phases, days of the week, gods and goddesses and the elements, so there are traditions linking different plants to different magical or ritual purposes.

It is important to note that the descriptions below are of magical symbolism and not medical prescriptions—medicinal herbalism is firmly based on medical research and study that takes many years and you should never prescribe herbs to yourself or others to apply physically or take internally without the appropriate medicinal training. There is some interesting crossover between medicinal herbalism and magical herbalism, but in practice they need to be kept safely separate!

Many witches like to make their own herbal oils.

The glossary refers to some of the most common plants used by witches for magical and ritual purposes. They are used in a variety of ways; as decoration for an altar, as part of an incense blend, in a balefire—a fire set for magical or ritual purposes, or as stuffing in cloth poppets, "fetishes" or manikins. Herbs can also be deployed in ritual or spell-work by anointing a candle with carrier oil and rolling it in the dried leaves and flowers.

Another use of herbs in magic is to place them in pouches to be tied to a bedpost or worn as a pendant around the neck. Hanging bunches or wreaths of herbs with protective or banishing properties around a hearth in the central point of a household, or at the front and back doors, is an old way of protecting your home. They can also be woven into chaplets to be placed around the base of ritual candles or into circlets to be worn on the heads of participants.

Some witches like to make their own herbed oil by steeping concentrated amounts of herb in a good oil, such as grapeseed, leaving it for at least a week to absorb the scent and energy of the leaves and then pouring the oil from the jar or bottle onto a fresh set of leaves. This process should be repeated until the oil is thoroughly scented with the herbal perfume. Particularly successful herbs for this treatment are rosemary, basil, sage and thyme. This oil is considered extra-charged for magical use as the magician has already placed their energy into its preparation for sacred purposes. Both the energy and intent of the maker infuse the oil with the type of energy that is helpful to spell-work.

However you decide to use the following herbal, try to grow your own or pick them from the wild. Fresh herbs give out a different vibe from dried (which can still be used at a pinch), and it is handy to have the fresh variety on hand. If you pick leaves and flowers from a plant, you should always ask the plant's permission—silently or aloud—and if it comes from the garden, bury a crumb of bread soaked with wine at its base as a thank-you to the Earth. If the glossary seems overloaded with

Fresh and dried herbs have different energies.

information, take heart from the fact that you are not expected to remember all of this at once and that this slice of knowledge can take a bunch of people a whole lifetime each to assemble.

FLORAL TYPES

Belladonna Also known as Deadly Nightshade, sacred to Lilith and Hecate, this is used in visionwork, banishings and bindings. Extremely poisonous and all precautions should be taken to prevent poisoning by contact.

Chamomile Used in a pillow to aid sleep and in incenses to aid meditation. Associated with success and money charms.

Honeysuckle symbolizes loyalty.

Carnation Sometimes known as clove flower, it is an energy-raiser and enhances the power of incense blends to which it is added. Also used in protection charms.

Cyclamen For love and protection; keeps nightmares at bay.

Geranium For use in love spells; good for countering anxiety and troubles of the mind.

Heliotrope Associated with solar deities, especially Apollo, heliotrope is used for prophecy and driving away negativity.

Lavender is one of the great "Universal" herbs.

Honeysuckle May be used at handfastings to symbolize loyalty. Is used in prosperity spells, and to heighten female sexual energy if picked the day after Full Moon.

Hyacinth Dedicated to Aphrodite, hyacinth is a plant of love and its scent is reputed to relieve grief and keep nightmares at bay. Used in healing and love spells.

Jasmine Having Earth and Moon correspondences, jasmine is associated with women's cycles and sometimes used in spells to aid in problems with menstruation or conception. Used in love spells to attract a true and passionate lover, as well as in prosperity spells in line with its Earthy aspect.

Lavender A herb associated with Air and Mercury, excellent in communication spells and used in combination with other flowers in love spells. Good in healing spells for skin ailments and troubles of the mind. Excellent in dream pillows to induce sleep and help the sleeper remember their dreams.

Lilac The fresh flowers are used to induce clear memories and to enhance path-working and trance-work. Used in love and healing spells.

Marigold A solar plant, used in healing and success incense blends. Also used in love charms and sometimes threaded into a necklace to wish a bride good luck at handfastings. Used to bring the healing life force to healing spells.

Marigolds have solar associations.

Poppy A lunar plant used to induce prophetic dreams and bring healing rest. Associated with female cycles, it aids fertility and conception and helps regulate monthly courses.

Rose Sacred to Aphrodite, the rose enhances love-oils and incense blends. Associated with Water, it is also good for healing charms.

Soloman's Seal For protection, cleansing and decision-making.

Yarrow Wards off negativity, is associated with Air functions such as travel.

Roses are sacred to the goddess of love.

You can use borage for courage.

HERBAL TYPES

Basil A variety of uses including purification, love and protection.

Borage The leaves and flowers of borage may be carried by those desiring courage and willpower in difficult situations. Promotes strength and endurance.

Catnip Famous for driving cats wild, it is used in love spells and is sacred to Bast and Sekhmet, the cat and lion-headed goddesses of Egypt. Used for driving out negativity.

Comfrey Also known as knitbone, comfrey is primarily a healing herb suitable for physical and mental ailments.

Eyebright For clear-seeing and prophecy; raises energy in all magical work.

Henbane Extremely poisonous and hazardous to handle. Used in exorcism and banishing as well as to induce visions. Never to be inhaled, applied or taken internally. All precautions should be taken to avoid poisoning through contact.

Horehound An earthy, sexy herb useful in fertility spells and for protection and prosperity.

Basil is used in purification rites.

Mint Prosperity, cleansing, healing, money-luck and love; this herb is a good multi-tasker.

Mugwort Sacred to Artemis and known as Artemesia; when the dried herb is burned it helps induce psychic visions. It drives cats wild, so best keep puss away! Keeps felons and false friends away from mischief.

Nettle Protection herb which can be burned or buried in a jar to protect a property and ward off gossip and hypocrites. A good antidote if someone is being spiteful. Excellent for banishing.

Mint has many magical associations.

Pennyroyal A lovely ground-hugging mint that is ideal for use in banishing bad feelings or envy that is directed toward you. Great for freshening old shoes, too!

Rosemary A common standby in the witches' herb cupboard, it has several magical functions including purification, protection and the preservation of memory. It can be used bunched together, to sprinkle the salt and water before a circle is cast, and grown at the doorway of a house for protection.

Rue Used for purification and good health; another multi-tasking standby to have close to hand.

Valerian Used to induce sleep. Also used in love-sachets.

SPICY TYPES

Asafoetida A nasty-smelling herb whose leaves are burned to drive away evil influences. Used in exorcism and guaranteed to drive everyone out!

Benzoin Gum used in incenses for success and a preservative against disaster.

Cinnamon Used to induce passion in men and for prosperity in business matters.

Nutmeg can be used for healing spells for elders.

Cloves For general good health and to attract others. Used in success incense blends and carried to draw lovers and keep trouble at bay.

Frankincense Protection and purification; sacred to the Sun and good for healing work.

Myrrh A gum used in purification incenses as well as for healing. Associated with burials and rebirth as well as protection.

Nutmeg Worn in a red pouch around the neck, can be used to draw good health and strength to the wearer. Particularly useful in healing spells for elders.

Cloves can be included in incense blends for success.

Orris The dried and powdered root of the iris is often used in love incense blends, but the perfume is pleasant enough to use it as a purification charm in the home. Can be placed in muslin sachets with oats and used in the bath along with lavender oil for a pre-ritual purification bath.

Patchouli A very earthy herb used to attract male sexual attention. Used in love oils and incenses, and as an Earth correspondence in prosperity mixes.

WOODY TYPES

Apple, Apple-blossom The apple tree is the gateway to the Celtic Otherworld, the abode of the Hag aspect of the goddess who ferries us from life to death and rebirth. Its leaves and blossoms are burned in trance-work, and love and healing spells.

Ash Leaves and branches are used for protection and prophecy.

Bay Leaves are burned for psychic work and clairvoyance as well as purification and healing.

Broom Associated with Air and wind, often used in weather magic. Also used for protection and purity.

Cypress For Underworld contacts such as Hecate or Dark Persephone; also used to consecrate magical tools. Smoke produced from its leaves promotes clairvoyance.

Dittany Very smoky if burned; powerful divination herb, aids decision-making and offers clear sight of a problem.

Eucalyptus is a good general healing herb.

Eucalyptus As well as being good for relieving sinus problems, it is a good general healing and protection herb with lunar associations.

Hawthorn Protection, beginnings and sexual desire. Good for getting projects moving and blasting through obstacles to progress.

Heather A weather herb, used to summon rain in dry spells and associated with protection. Sacred to the Goddess.

Hawthorn is a fairy flower that is associated with Beltane.

Holly With its prickly leaves, holly is a herb of protection; its berries can be threaded and used to hold an oath-maker to their promise.

Juniper A major force for protection in magical terms; often used to deter thieves or intruders, loops of the threaded berry can be hung in the home at doors and windows. A protective herb, the dried berries can be used alone as a purification incense. Good for banishing and binding spells as well as protection against mishap when traveling.

Mandrake Its root is used in fertility spells and for reviving sexual desire in men; since it is rare, White Betony is sometimes used in its place. It is also a protective plant and when buried by a gatepost is said to keep intruders or unwanted visitors away.

Mistletoe Protection, fertility and amity. Used in amulets for general protection, it is reputed, possibly through its association with the oak tree, to guard against lightning and so is sometimes placed in the porch of tall houses. Also used in spells to heal rifts in friendships.

Myrtle A wonderfully scented herb, it grows wild in the Mediterranean and the mature plant resembles a tree or bush if left to grow. Sacred to Astarte, myrtle is useful in spells to promote passion in a lover and for love and fertility. The wood is particularly good for carving love-charms. A good herb to have along at a handfasting.

Rowan Apparently guards against witches(!) but is a good protective plant; the berries can be used to seal bargains and protect property. Can also be burned for divination.

Wormwood Used in divinatory work and for protection.

Oils and incenses

The use of scent in ritual can be a powerful aid to spiritual development and spell-work, with different perfumes promoting mood changes and altered states of consciousness. They help open the door to the emotions and memory and from there tap into our deepest selves—the spark within connected with and part of the divine. Both essential oils and incenses capture the essence of a plant and thus carry the concentrated energy of a plant's magical and spiritual properties. They can be used to good effect in circle- and meditation-work in a variety of ways.

Oils are particularly versatile. Only pure essential oils should be used for circle-work as these are natural essences encapsulating the plant qualities. Inferior "perfumed" oils may be cheaper, but often contain chemical contaminants and probably have never even been waved near the

It is now common for people to have oil burners at home.

plants whose scents they attempt to mimic! Essential oils can be used in burners in the place of incense; they can also be used to anoint candles and help charge them with their energy, plus the energy of our intent and power-raising. Diluted essential oils can be used to anoint people for self-blessing—the level of concentration is particularly crucial here (see Warnings section on page 339). They can also be used to scent pre-circle bath sachets for purification or mood-setting, or added to sticky incense blends.

If you are using an oil burner, note that the essential oil is usually added to water placed in the dish above a lit tealight. If you intend using essential oil diluted with carrier oil such as grapeseed or almond, either for anointing a person or a candle, ensure that the dilute proportions are within safe limits. You will also need to keep a dry towel close at hand, as oil spreads very quickly and can make hands and implements very slippery.

USING INCENSE

The use of incense in circles, particularly loose incense, can be dramatic and add to the atmosphere of the sacred space. They can be used with certain herbs (see pages 329–330) to promote the altered states of consciousness that participants seek to achieve. Echoing the practices of our pagan ancestors, incense carries our wishes to the deities on the sweet, airborne smoke.

Loose incense is the best to use, blended for the specific purpose of circle-, divination- or meditation-work. Although single ingredient incenses are used sometimes, such as juniper berries for purification or dittany for divination, in Wiccan circles blends are more common. Some people have a particular gift for blending beautiful incenses—but the craft of blending is not difficult to learn if you gather a few basics together from the glossary on pages 340–341. Incenses commonly comprise gums such as frankincense, myrrh, copal or benzoin; a base such as white or red sandalwood; dried herbs, flowers and/or berries; and occasionally essential oils or even store-cupboard ingredients such as honey, dried fruit or wine. For blending, you will need a clean working surface such as a marble chopping board, a pestle and mortar and some jars for storage. A sharp knife, or better still a double-handled herb chopper, is a real boon for preparation.

A supply of bottles and droppers are very useful aids to blending oils.

DEVELOPING SKILLS AND KNOWLEDGE

The benefit of using loose incense is that you can create special blends suited to the particular purposes of the ritual work you are undertaking. Different blends can be created for different Moon phases and Sabbats, as well as blends for elemental work and specific types of spells. One of the most beautiful I ever used was an evocative blend produced by a friend for the autumn equinox, and smelled of orchards and ancient temples. The blends should be created at the appropriate Moon phase in order to capture the energies you wish to release when the incense is burned. The loose blends are burned on a red-hot charcoal disc, which can be purchased at alternative shops and over the internet. These are placed in fire-proof censers which in turn are placed on a fire-proof mat to prevent scorch damage to floors and furniture.

Warnings

If you are pregnant, have high blood pressure or suffer from any serious health problems, you are strongly advised to consult a medical practitioner or therapist before using any of the following oils or incense ingredients. All essential oils need to be diluted before they can be used on the skin or in the bath; some essential oils are not appropriate for use in this way. These very powerful essences have physical effects and should be treated with great respect.

Diluted oil for anointing objects or persons should never be more concentrated than 7 drops of essential oil to 1 tablespoon of carrier oil (grapeseed, almond or olive oil), and care should be taken at all times to keep oil away from the eyes.

Glossary of oils and incenses

Please note that the majority of essential oils, woods or gums carry the properties ascribed to their herb, flower or plant; the ones included here refer either to properties particular to their oil or, in the case of wood or gum, have not been already mentioned in the witches' herbal (see pages 324–335).

ESSENTIAL OILS

Almond Carrier oil but used for prosperity and fertility blends in its own right.

Basil Uplifting, for clearing the head and preventing tension and conflict.

Bergamot Uplifting, healing and purification, inspiration.

Clove Stirs the passions, takes away pain, summons sweet memories.

Geranium Aids appetite in convalescents, love, harmony, relaxation, stress-breaker.

Ginger Passion, digestive problems, breaks through lethargy.

Lavender Induces sleep, relaxation, healing.

Lemongrass Spiritual development, clairvoyance, healing.

Rose absolute Love, harmony, healing. Rose absolute is extremely expensive; geranium is a good substitute.

Ginger oil is a lively antidote to lethargy.

Lemongrass aids clairvoyance.

Sandalwood Protection, healing, consecration, blessing.

Tea-tree Purification, banishing, exorcism.

Vanilla Restores vigor, energy, aphrodisiac, warms the senses.

Violet Love, healing, balancing the emotions.

Ylang-ylang Aphrodisiac par excellence! Promotes prophetic dreams.

WOODS, GUMS AND PLANTS

Cedar Prosperity, inheritance, domestic matters, tradition.

Cinnamon Health, passion, raising energy.

Copal Purification, banishing, binding.

Henna Blessing, honoring the God and Goddess within, tradition.

Pine Purification, communication, renewal.

Red sandalwood Harmony, drawing energy, common base for incense blends.

White sandalwood Spiritual blessings, consecrations, blessings, purification, common base for incense blends.

Incense blends

The following recipes are a selection of standard basic blends for circle and spell-work.

Love

Blend all ingredients together on a waxing Moon, to draw love.

½ teaspoon powdered orris root

I teaspoon rose petals

½ teaspoon myrrh

I teaspoon honeysuckle

½ teaspoon white sandalwood

½ teaspoon honey

I teaspoon chopped raisins

Initiation

Blend all ingredients together at Dark Moon.

½ teaspoon dittany

9 drops cypress oil

I teaspoon frankincense

½ teaspoon myrrh

I teaspoon rowan berries

Purification

Blend all ingredients together as the Moon wanes.

I teaspoon white sandalwood

½ teaspoon copal

9 drops carnation oil

9 cloves

I teaspoon mistletoe

½ teaspoon mandrake root

PROSPERITY

Blend all ingredients together as the Moon waxes, for increase.

3 bay leaves

3 mint leaves

6 drops clove oil

½ teaspoon poppyseeds

1 teaspoon honeysuckle

½ teaspoon cedar

Incenses are very powerful tools in magical work.

DIVINATION

Blend all ingredients together at the Dark Moon.

1 teaspoon dittany

1 teaspoon crushed bay leaves

1 teaspoon mugwort

3 drops cypress oil

1 teaspoon red sandalwood

3 drops lemongrass oil

MOON CIRCLE

Blend all ingredients together on a waxing Moon.

2 teaspoons frankincense

1 teaspoon white sandalwood

½ teaspoon juniper berries

3 drops geranium oil

½ teaspoon powdered orris root

2 teaspoons dried rosemary

Trees and tree lore

Wicca is a nature religion, and we often refer to non-human beings such as animals, rocks and plants as our relations. Nowhere is this affinity with nature more apparent than our relationship with trees. We know that our ancestors honored the spirits of trees and that certain trees had magical, spiritual and divine associations. The impulse to "touch wood" or "knock on wood" for

Trees carry environmental history records within them.

Superstitions about wood and trees are evidence of ancient tree lore.

luck comes from ancient beliefs regarding the sacred nature of trees, as do certain traditions regarding Christmas trees and Yuletide logs. The many old folk traditions about trees and certain types of wood are connected with much older beliefs about tree-spirits, and often what appears to be superstition is actually a remnant of ancestral memory.

Trees are amazing plants. They register in their growth patterns historical, meteorological and geological upheavals, and can live for hundreds of years. Trees provide homes, shelter and shade for insect, animal and other plant life, and are the lungs of our planet. When they die or are cut down, they provide material to build and make beautiful our own habitat.

UNIVERSAL SYMBOL

Trees also provide us with spiritual lessons; rooted in the strong foundation of Earth, they grow toward the sky, connecting heaven and earth and belonging to both. They respond to the seasons, shedding and sleeping in winter, to prepare for rebirth in the following spring. It is not surprising that the Tree of Life is such a universal symbol of spiritual aspiration and development. Our Norse ancestors conceived of a great ash tree, Ygdrasil, as an expression of all existence; indeed trees play an important part in many ancient creation myths. The Celts were great tree-lovers and, in common with ancient Greek religionists, used protected sacred groves of trees as outdoor temples and ritual space.

Stories of the ancient gods and goddesses are dotted with tree references; in ancient Egyptian legends Osiris's coffin finds its way into, variously, a pine or tamarisk tree. Daphne, chased by Apollo, is turned into a laurel, while the goddess Athena gives the gift of the olive tree to the Greeks. In the Judeo-Christian mythology, knowledge comes to humankind through the fruit of the apple tree. The importance of trees to our civilization and the stories attached to them cannot be overemphasized.

TREE ALPHABET

The Celts had such a strong affinity with trees that they invented a tree alphabet, the *Beth-Luis-Nion*, sometimes *Beth-Luis-Fearn*. These have links to a 13-month calendar—each month beginning at New Moon. All the letters are related to a shrub or tree, and those born in the lunar month relating to that tree are said to bear some of its qualities, rather like the zodiac signs in astrology. In addition, there is a system of divination related to the Ogham symbols of the alphabet, cast rather like the runes (see pages 350–357).

The following glossary is indicative only and there are variations in interpretation and correspondence. Further understanding of the system can be achieved through study, meditation and direct contact with the trees themselves.

As your studies progress, you will gain a working knowledge of the deeper meanings of the patterns in the alphabet.

CREE ALPHABEC

Letter	Tree	Characteristics
B Beth	Birch	Discipline, determination, organization
L Luis	Rowan	Protection, swift growth, aspiration
N Nion	Ash	Magic, the mysteries, gateway, intellect
F Fearn	Alder	Divination, crafts, wisdom, regeneration
S Saille	Willow	Psychic power, healing, tides of magic and dreams
H Uath	Hawthorn	Protection, love, fertility, door to the Celtic Otherworld
D Duir	Oak	Strength, protection, courage, health, spiritual integrity and service
T Tinne	Holly	Protection, oath-keeping, joy, life-force, wisdom
C Coll	Hazel	Fertility, intuition, nurture, longevity
M Muin	Vine	Ecstasy, shamanism, sensuality, happiness, rebellion
G Gort	Ivy	Loyalty, regeneration, fidelity, trust
P Pelboc	Dwarf	Service to others, healing, defense, intrepidness
R Ruis	Elder	Rebirth, consecration, generative principle, daring
A Ailm	Silver fir	Purity, hope, clear-sightedness, shrewdness
O Onn	Gorse	Relationships, home, love-matches, friendship, principles
U Ur	Heather	Promise, steadfastness, artistic ability, love of tradition
E Eadha	White	Time, longevity, self-determination, knowledge
I Idho	Yew	Guardianship, flexibility, doorway, ancestors

TREE FOLKLORE

There are many sayings in folklore concerning trees, some of which contain little nuggets of wisdom. The superstition that one should never burn alder, because the Old Gal—another name for the tree, referring to its goddess associations—is actually good advice because it crackles and spits and is something of a safety hazard! Other sayings have a similarly practical element: For example, the notion that "Oak draws the stroke, ash the flash" comes from the fact that these trees are likely to be the tallest in the wood and therefore more likely to be struck by lightning. The advice to crawl under the

Acorns are associated with solar energy and god-forms.

hawthorn instead is probably sound, as the height and spread of hawthorn is restricted in woodland settings and therefore less susceptible to lightning strikes.

Some trees have specific planetary, elemental and divine associations. The oak is strongly associated with the Green Man, Jack-in-the-Green and Robin Hood/Goodfellow, and Herne or Cernunnos, the Horned God and guardian of the forest. It is linked with solar energy and the Fire element and is especially sacred to Druids, whose name is thought to come from the old name for oak, *duir*. The willow has strong lunar and Water connections, and is sacred to the Old One—the Hag aspect of the triple Goddess. Willow is associated with magic, dreams and psychic power, and wands made from its wood are

DEVELOPING SKILLS AND KNOWLEDGE

particularly popular with women. The ash has Earth and Air associations, reflecting its interconnecting qualities. Ash wood, dyed or painted black, is a popular choice in the Wiccan community for athame handles. It is considered to be a powerful protection and a conduit for two-way energy, again reflecting the Earth-sky links of the ash tree.

Hawthorn could probably command a whole book of its own in terms of spiritual and magical connotations; it is considered a Fairy tree, guarding the gateway to the Otherworld, and folks are warned not to fall asleep beneath them. In some parts of Europe contractors have been forced to change building plans because of the refusal of workers to uproot ancient hawthorns. They are sacred to Cardea, Roman goddess of gateways, fertility and change, and the blossoming of the hawthorn marks Beltane, the first Sabbat of the summer. Its protective qualities encouraged people to bring it indoors to bless the house. At some point, however, this was reconstructed as drawing bad luck rather than good, probably to discourage pagan practices. Consequently, it is now considered lucky to bring hawthorn blossom indoors only on the feast of Beltane.

Should you ever wish to cut a wand from a living tree, be sure to ask its permission first and thank it after. I speak as one who was once careless while gathering holly and gained a permanent scar in the shape of "Ken" reversed for my trouble (see page 355).

In some cultures, the cutting of particular trees is considered to draw bad luck.

Runes

R unes are letters of an ancient Germanic alphabet developed over the last two millennia to form 24 symbols, and these were used to keep records. The characters are formed from straight lines, reflecting their early origins when they were carved into stone or wood. The runes also carried meaning beyond their written or phonetic usage; they embodied esoteric knowledge and power and were used for divination and magic.

Runes are symbols of a system developed over two thousand years.

The word *rune* means mystery or secret, and each symbol embodies a spiritual concept. Norse myth holds that Odin, the All-Father, brought the secret of the runes at great cost to himself; he underwent a form of shamanic initiation by hanging upside down from the world tree, the Ash Ygdrasil, for nine days and nights in order to gain knowledge of their secrets. He won the runes, the knowledge of which endowed him with power and wisdom. Odin passed this knowledge to Freya, goddess of the *seidr* or "vision magic," and eventually Hagal, god of the rainbow connecting Middle Earth and the home of the gods, passed runic knowledge to humankind.

The Old German rune alphabet is sometimes called the "Elder Futhark," the word *Futhark* comprising its first six letters. The Anglo-Saxon version or *Futhorc* contains 33 symbols owing to linguistic differences in the regions to which its use spread. The Futhark is the most commonly used system. It is divided into thee Aetts, each a set of eight symbols. The first Aett are dedicated to Freya, the second to Hagal and the third to Tyr, god of courage and defense, and the meanings attached to them reflect this (see charts on pages 355–357).

Most Wiccans, delighted to have a living record of a genuinely ancient magical system, put the runes to several uses. They are a useful way to express and symbolize specific spiritual values and so we sometimes wear them as pendants to draw their power. Witches also use runes for divination purposes: casting a set of rune-stones or discs randomly and divining the meanings from the shapes, patterns, order and direction in which they land; or drawing them at random and laying them in spreads rather like the Tarot. As with the Tarot, runic divination is a means by which to discern patterns and act upon them, rather than being a tool for "fortune-telling." The symbols themselves carry a good deal of power, however, so if you choose to use runes for divination purposes, you should treat them respectfully and take heed of what they tell you.

Another use for the runes in Wicca is in spell-work. It is useful to have a set of characters that symbolize different spiritual concepts in sympathetic magic; the runes provide an effective means by which we can summon the appropriate energies, précis our intent and focus on the desired outcomes with brevity. They carry their own concentrated power, beyond the function of symbolism, and witches often find that working with them over time enhances intuition and magical abilities.

RUNES AND MEDITATION

Runes are also used in meditation work; a favorite method is to hold a rune in your power-hand (usually your writing hand), close your eyes and trace the carved line of its character with your fingertips as you allow your attention to sink within yourself. Messages and insights derived from this freeform method of meditation come from the rune itself, which imprints itself on your conscious and sub-conscious states kinetically, through touch, during your inner journey. A more directed method can be used however; this works by focusing on a particular problem and selecting a rune that you feel suits this problem; for example, Daeg, the rune of clear-seeing, can help you find the truth of a situation. You ask the rune a direct question relating to the problem and see what comes into your mind. The runes are not always direct, the answer may come in hints, random thoughts or symbols, but intuition is primary in rune-work, and you will have to practice and work with the runic system in order to get the best results from this method of seeing. Many people like to use divinatory incense alongside this type of meditation (see page 343).

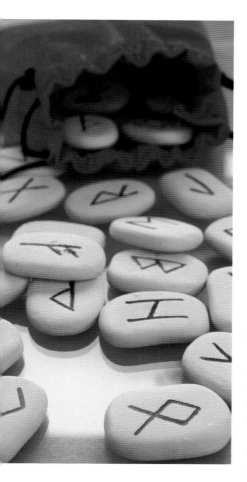

Making your own set is an excellent self-development project.

Although sets of runes are available for purchase from alternative outlets nowadays, it is possible to make your own set. You can do this by gathering suitable stones from a river-bed and painting them, or by dividing a branch of even thickness into 24 discs and carving the symbols into them. If you choose the latter method, you will find it useful to refer back to the list of correspondences on page 347 in order to choose the most appropriate tree for your purposes. A favored choice, given the legendary origins of the runes, is ash. However, everyone has their favorite tree and style of magic and many different woods are used to make rune sets. If you do take wood from a living tree, try to do so outside of the growing season, ensure that you ask permission of the tree, leave payment (in other words, give back), and use an organic sealant on the wound to prevent infection from getting in through the unprotected wood.

Runic systems

The single meaning of a rune should be considered in the context of the Aett to which it belongs. Freya's Aett is influenced by her divine characteristics. As she is goddess of love, nurture, pleasure and joy, Freya's runes are imbued with these qualities and should be seen in that light. Hagal, guardian of the bridge linking Middle Earth and the home of the gods, brings to his Aett the influences of achievement, material matters, earthly power and success. Tyr, a mighty warrior god, renowned for his courage and protective powers, brings to his Aett all of the concerns of the protector, including justice, fairness, matters of authority, decision-making and moral redemption.

When working with the runes, try to understand their spiritual meaning by placing them within the context of the Aett in which they are grouped. It is also helpful to regard the following as a starting point, rather than a definitive explanation of what the runes represent or their purpose. All mysteries are multi-layered, and the themes and influences of the runes will unfold to you if you take the time to research, study and practice working with them, treating them with respect.

The following is a list of the Elder Futhark, divided into the three Aetts. The names of the runes vary according to different systems—the ones used here are standard Old Germanic with a common popular rendition in brackets. There is, apparently, no historical precedent for the blank rune—Odin's rune—which was introduced in the late twentieth century. However, this can be interpreted as another development along the way of what has been a process of development for the runes. Although the characters and their names are genuinely ancient, the meanings ascribed to them today are framed by modern interpretation for a modern world.

Freya's Aett

Rune	Name	Symbol	Characteristics and meanings
ᚠ	Fehu (Feoh) F	Cattle	Wealth, redistribution, gathering one's energies
ᚢ	Uruz (Ur) U	Aurochs	Strength, unavoidable change, the will, challenge
ᚦ	Thurisaz (Thorn) TH	Thorn	Protection, obstacles overcome, generosity
ᚨ	Ansuz (Ansur) A	Mouth	Speech, communication, movement, progress, passing tests
ᚱ	Raidho (Rad) R	Wheel	Journeys, path to spiritual fulfilment, surprises, good news, change in fortune, negotiations
ᚲ	Kenaz (Ken) K/C	Knowledge	Wisdom, light, heeding life lessons, proposals, healing, recovery, fire
ᚷ	Gebo (Gyfu) G	Gift	Love, partnership, goodwill, gifts, sacrifice rewarded
ᚹ	Wunjo (Wynn) W/V	Joy	Happiness, laughter, good news, awaited results

hagal's aett

Rune	Name	Symbol	Characteristics and meanings
ᚼ	Hagalaz (Hagal) H	Hail	Natural forces, balance, unification, reconciliation, obstacles, needed change
ᚾ	Nauthiz (Nid) N	Need	Necessity, constraint, patience, sorrow, biding one's time, adversity
ᛁ	Isa (Is) I	Ice	Stalemate, isolation, stillness, standstill, holding position, keeping one's counsel
ᛃ	Jera (Jara) J/Y	Year	Cycles, harvest, completion, results, deeds revisited, reward, work that is finished
ᛇ	Eihwaz (Yr) EI	Yew	Defense, averting disaster, flexibility, the ancestors, ancient wisdom
ᛈ	Perthro (Peorth) P	Dice cup	Chance, good luck, good fortune, secrets, the recovery of things feared lost, the unexpected
ᛉ	Elhaz (Eolh) Z	Elk	Peace, defense, friendship, banishing care, the ability to evolve, personal changes
ᛋ	Sowilo (Sigil) S	Sun	Health, wholeness, life-force, success, poetry and music

Tyr's Aett

Rune	Name	Symbol	Characteristics and meanings
↑	Tiwaz (Tiw) T	God Tyr	Energy, power, victory, success, spiritual quest
ᛒ	Berkano (Beorc) B	Birch	Cleansing, growth, fertility, discipline, patience, fairness, interpersonal skills
ᛖ	Ehwaz (Eoh) E	Horse	Journeys, gradual changes, growth, communication, new places
ᛗ	Mannaz (Mann) M	Humans	Humanity, dignity, self-esteem, love for humankind, cooperation, justice, integrity
ᛚ	Laguz (Lagu) L	Water	Women's cycles, pregnancy, flow and process, conduits, dreams, psychic matters, a journey
◇	Ingwaz (Ing) NG	God Freyr	Fertility, family, harmonious relationships, beginnings, domestic property, consolidation
ᛞ	Dagaz (Daeg) D	Day	Insight, clarity, truth, radical positive change, wonder, appreciation of beauty
ᛟ	Othala (Othal) O	Property	Inheritance, material and spiritual legacy, separation, preservation of custom and law

Myths and stories

Because Wicca is a diverse spirituality there is no single body of mythology that embodies the whole of our tradition of story and myth. We find significance in many ancient tales and are not afraid of reinventing or reinterpreting them in the time-honored fashion of successive generations.

One of the best-known Wiccan stories is the "Myth of the Goddess," which is sometimes enacted in rituals for initiates. This story involves the descent of the Goddess to the Underworld to learn the secret of Death. She is forced to cast aside, at each gate, all her worldly accoutrements until she stands naked. Finally, she is embraced by Death, who reveals the secret knowledge that she seeks. The interpretation of this tale is left to the initiate, who, like the Goddess, stands at the gate ready to step into the unknown, willing to put aside convention and distraction in order to make themselves fit to learn that which is worth knowing.

MANY MYTHS OF THE GODDESS

This myth is a modern rendition of a combination of several ancient stories of goddesses descending to the Underworld. The oldest of these is the descent of Innanna, the intrepid goddess of ancient Sumeria, who with cunning, initiative, compassion and self-sacrifice descends, leaving her accoutrements, jewels and clothes at the seven gates to the land of the Dead. In the Underworld, she suffers in order to gain knowledge and returns to the upper world with the power and wisdom she set out to find.

There are also echoes of the story of Persephone, daughter of the Earth Goddess Demeter, which may have evolved from the Innanna cycle. The Maiden Goddess Persephone descends to the Underworld and, because she eats six pomegranate seeds while there, is forced to return for six months each year, during which time her divine mother mourns and neglects the Earth's greenery, thus causing seasonal ebb and flow. Both legends have strong solar themes, the

Dimitte q̃ fe veiule z mouues | fouudoit de fon troſne ſuſubu
...retout des auaeiens relint | reur q̃ſe fleuures z aſſes pꝛeſ
uſigure. Deſtall coe ſua ea | ſuut auaut ralu uotable loſ
...reble houre ſeaud eu ſua ſiſt | quels ſout ꝑ uoutes ffuia
ſuruxx theoſte q̃ en ſa mau | bleut la roiuc deufer pſepie
reuou ſuut ropuſ ceptre et | auſlee dout la fare eſt teible
ſouibs ſee pieds auoit ſoug | coe femme pluto ſcad iouure

The story of Persephone is part of an ancient mythology related to the solar cycle.

notion of the descent or fall of the Sun's powers in the course of the year's cycle. The emphasis on the descent of a goddess rather than a god indicates ancient links made between the regenerative powers of the Sun to a goddess; perhaps the association of the rise and fall of the light with the male principal came much later.

DEVELOPING SKILLS AND KNOWLEDGE

THE OAK AND HOLLY KINGS

There is a Wiccan tradition linking different aspects of the god to seasonal change. This is based on the folk custom of a fight between the Oak and the Holly kings. The Holly King is the lord of the waning year, a winter version of the Green Man. He is a nature spirit whose message is hope in the depths of winter and in Wicca he represents, among other things, maturity. The Oak King is the newcomer, a rival to the Holly King, as his rule is based on the rising of the light rather than the period of stillness that comes when the days are darker.

The battles between the Oak and Holly kings, symbolizing the predominance of either light or darkness, are not fought at any of the solar festivals—solstices and equinoxes—but at Beltane (for the affections of the Goddess, ostensibly) and at Samhain, respectively the first festivals of Summer and Winter. The outcome of the battles is a foregone conclusion, as the winner will be the one who is set to predominate at that time of year. However, this knowledge has never stopped the very determined from strapping on antlers and combat gear and attempting to knock the stuffing out of their opponent.

ARTHUR'S LEGEND

Elements of the partnership between goddess and god are seen in the Arthurian legends in Wiccan interpretations of them. The Arthurian cycle casts the hero as young god (conceived under mysterious circumstances), shaman (apprenticed to Merlin and initiated by the Lady of the Lake) and consort to the goddess of sovereignty (King of the Land). The fate of the solar god is reflected in Arthur's story; he is mortally wounded, yet remains undying as he is taken away to Avalon—the Isle of Apples (fruit of the Celtic Otherworld)—by, variously, three or nine maidens, a reference to the Triple Goddess. There are parallels with the journey of the waning Sun, descending lower in the sky each day after the autumn equinox. The

Foliage masks are modeled on the Green Man, who sometimes manifests as both Oak King and Holly King

dying Sun-god journeys to the land of the Dead, where he sojourns with the Goddess, Mother of all living things, to be restored and eventually reborn when his light rises higher over the horizon after the winter solstice. Of course, if we do not happen to see the Sun as male or the God aspect of God and Goddess as the Sun, this parallel is of little significance. However, there is no denying the references in Arthurian legend to the issue of the marriage between Arthur, symbol of divine origins within human frailty, and the Earth.

For those of us who perceive deity as female—the male residing within female or who perceive God and Goddess as aspects of the One without the constraints of gendered role models—there is another story to be found in the cycle of the year. This moves us beyond the rise and fall of the Sun and into a far richer interpretation of seasonal and life changes.

At Imbolc, the Maiden Goddess grows toward womanhood in the company of women. At the same time, the young God grows in the love of his parents, raised in the greenwood, learning and exploring its ways. By Eostre, the Maiden has grown to womanhood and the young God to early manhood; they become lovers and conceive a child. At Beltane, they set aside their wild days to handfast beneath the hawthorn blossom. Both shed their antlers, symbols of growth and change, and take on the mantle of responsibility. Through the summer, they reign in splendor, storing the strength of the Sun to carry them into the dark part of the year.

At Lammas comes the corn harvest, and the spirit of John Barleycorn—an aspect of the God—is captured in corn dollies to ensure his return the following year, as spirit of regeneration. At Samhain, the pregnant Goddess is attended by her own elder self, the Hag, and both she and the God depart to the darker shores of the Dreamtime to prepare for the rebirth of the God at the winter solstice, and thus the cycle begins again.

If you are wondering where this story begins and ends, how the Goddess got to be a Hag at the same time as she is a Maiden and a Mother, you are missing the point. The cycle of the year, like the story, is about constant changes, not neat endings and absolute beginnings. And this is why stories, subject to many levels of interpretation, are the ideal vehicle for expressing something of the way that Wicca approaches the essential truths—the big questions—about the nature of the Universe and our place within it.

The Arthurian cycle is replete with ancient archetypes.

RITUALS
AND
CEREMONIES

key rituals

Wicca has evolved traditions to mark life changes.

A s you may have already gathered, there is far more to ritual work than spells. Seasonal changes are celebrated at the eight Sabbats, the major festivals of the Wiccan year. The changing phases of the Moon are celebrated at Esbats, when we gather to honor the God and Goddess, to cast spells and to work on our own spiritual and magical development. The Sabbats and Esbats carry a personal element—as we celebrate seasonal and cyclical change in the world around us, we consider how these might be reflected in our own lives. However, there are rituals that relate far more directly to the personal; rituals that help us to mark life events and celebrate rites of passage.

Why perform a ritual? The significance of marking life-cycle or life-changing events with ritual in Wicca is that by enacting change symbolically within a sacred space, we send a message to our deepest spiritual selves, with the deities as witnesses. While in the circle we are working between the worlds, weaving new patterns that are registered in the great web of existence. Because we are working symbolically, we are accessing our deeper consciousness. The effect of this dual impact brings about psychological and spiritual affirmation of the changes that have happened or are about to take place.

A word of advice; it is possible to over-ritualize different aspects of our lives needlessly and this tendency is usually checked by the kindly counsel of a sister or brother practitioner early in our development in the Craft. It really isn't necessary to have a ritual for every single event, for example, before we leave the house or eat or make a decision. In addition, rituals do not have to be elaborate, in fact, the simpler, the more effective, as a rule.

The following rituals are examples of ceremonies that you can perform for different key life-cycle events. They are designed to enable guests to be directly involved in the ceremony and can be adjusted accordingly. The basic structure assumes that you will be working with others within a cast circle, with officers for the elements who will light their respective candles when they have welcomed their element. All rituals in this section are very basic examples and can be easily recast to reflect your needs and preferences.

Life-cycle rituals commemorate changes in our inner and outer worlds.

Naming ceremony

This ritual is designed to enable friends and relatives to get involved at various stages of the ceremony, so agree beforehand who is to do what.

RITUAL

You will need

- An officer for each element
- Purification incense such as frankincense
- Chalice of water
- Loaf of bread
- Circlet of flowers for baby's head
- White candles in secure holders for each guest

Performing the ritual

1 Light incense and cast a circle.

2 Officer for Air says: "I welcome to this circle the element of Air with all its blessings. [To the baby] May you be blessed with learning and knowledge, with wit and the power to communicate easily with others."

Officer for Fire says: "I welcome to this circle the element of Fire with all its blessings. May you be blessed with courage, the will and the strength to work for what is right."

3 Officer for Water says: "I welcome to this circle the element of Water with all its blessings. May you be blessed with love and friendship, and the gift of intuition." Officer for Earth says: "I welcome to this circle the element of Earth and all its blessings. May you be blessed with health, prosperity and knowledge of your roots in the Earth." Officer for Spirit says: "I welcome to this circle the element of Spirit and all its blessings. May you be blessed with wisdom and use your gifts to make the world a better place as you grow."

Naming ceremonies are found in many cultures.

4 The parent(s) then say: "We are here to welcome a new baby to our family and our community, to ask that the Goddess watches over this little one and witnesses our wishes for her/him. [Speaking to the baby, placing the circlet on his/her head] We/I name you [name]. Welcome." All those present say: "Welcome [name]."

5 A chosen guest places a crumb of bread into the baby's hand, saying: "May you never hunger and may you always have enough to share." [To guests] "May all present honor the trust that [baby] places in us as she/he grows."

6 Another chosen guest wets the baby's lips with water from the chalice, saying: "May you never thirst and may you always have enough to share." [To guests] "May all present see this child raised with love."

7 All guests step forward in turn to offer their wishes for the little one, lighting a candle to seal their wish and placing it in the centre of the circle before stepping way.

8 The parent(s) thank all the guests, the element officers thank the elements and the circle-caster disperses the circle.

handfasting

This ceremony is traditionally for a year and a day, but here the commitment is for "as long as love lasts," a common Wiccan vow. The ceremony outlined below is for different- or same-sex couples. You can incorporate readings or songs by friends and relatives. An exchange of rings is mentioned but you can forgo this and simply exchange promises. It is usual to use one's initiation cords to bind your hands, but new cord can be used and kept in a safe place afterward.

A pagan wedding is known as a handfasting.

RITUAL

You will need

- Love-incense (see page 342) lit prior to circle-casting
- Bread
- Chalice of wine or juice
- Cord
- Broomstick

Performing the ritual

1 Cast a circle.

2 Officer for Air says: "I welcome the element of Air which brings to this circle and this marriage the gifts of communication and good memories." Officer for Fire says: "I welcome the element of fire which brings to this circle and this marriage the gifts of loyalty and passion." Officer for

Water says: "I welcome the element of Water which brings to this circle and this marriage the gift of love and patience."

3 Officer for Earth says: "I welcome the element of Earth which brings to this circle and this marriage the gifts of stability and a firm foundation." Officer for Spirit says: "I welcome the element of Spirit which brings to this circle and this marriage the gifts of wise choices in all that you do for and say to each other."

4 Partner 1 says: "Before this company, in this place and at this time I come to pledge my commitment to [name of Partner 2]." Partner 2 then says "Before this company, in this place and at this time I come to pledge my commitment to [name of Partner 1]."

5 A chosen guest breaks a piece of bread in half and offers a piece to each partner, saying: "May you never know want and always share what you have." Another chosen guest

offers each partner wine/juice from a chalice, saying: "May you drink from the same cup and always remember the love you expressed for each other on this day/night."

6 Partner 1 to 2 says: "[Name] I offer this ring, symbol of unity, with love and in trust and as a sign of my commitment to you." Partner 2 repeats the same phrase.

7 Both partners wrap the cord around the wrists of their joined hands and, looking at each other, say in unison: "I bind myself to you of my free will, I will honor your right to change and to grow, and I will support and love you in the best way I can, for as long as love lasts. So mote it be!"

8 Both partners jump over the broomstick. The handfasting is complete and the party can begin.

Croning/Wiseman ceremony

A Croning or Wiseman ceremony marks our entry into that phase of life when we have grown a little wiser by spending a certain number of years on the planet. For women, the ceremony is usually set post-menopause, which is a process rather than a distinct cutoff point. Entering elderhood for men is similarly about process and judging when to mark the changes.

This ritual has traditionally become a party at which friends offer gifts and praise elderhood. The ritual outlined below provides space for friends to come forward with poems, gifts and insights as part of the celebration. Like all group circles, there should be an officer for each element and an officer to crown the Crone/Wiseman.

RITUAL

You will need

- Bunches of dried sage for smudging (purifying space/people)
- Crown of fresh sage and rosemary

Performing the ritual

1 Cast a circle.

2 Officer for Air says: "Blowing from the east, the winds of change. Riding through the Air on brooms, the Hags of the East. Hail

Croning ceremonies honor the wisdom of older women.

and welcome!" [All respond] "Hail and welcome!"

3 Officer for Fire says: "Out of the flames the Phoenix rises, old and young and wise, strength and courage remade. Hail and welcome!" [All respond] "Hail and welcome!"

4 Officer for Water says: "Rain, puddles, streams, rivers, seas and the mighty oceans, all part of the great cycle. Hail and welcome!" [All respond] "Hail and welcome!"

5 Officer for Earth says: "Gaia, eldest, in whom all is dispersed and all is renewed. Hail and welcome!" [All respond] "Hail and welcome!"

6 Crowning officer to Crone/Wiseman says: "[Name] We have gathered to honor you as you enter elderhood and to name you Crone/Wiseman, sage and honored elder. The silver in your hair comes from time spent under the Moon, the knowledge in your counsel from treading the path before others and the wisdom in your hands from weaving the web which is the source of life for us now and for those to come. Hail and be honored, Crone/Wiseman." [Smudges elder with smoldering dried sage leaves before placing the crown on his/ her head]

7 Friends come forward one by one, to read poems to the elder and offer praise and gifts.

8 Crowning officer to Crone/Wiseman: "Honored one, know that the gift of age is wisdom. May you offer that wisdom kindly and carefully, and with patience. Remember always to recognize beauty and strength in the changes that time has brought to your body. Defy convention and embody nothing that is not your true self. Blessed Be." [All respond] "Blessed Be!"

Circle-name ceremony

When you have chosen a magical or circle-name you will need to introduce yourself by this name to the elements and the God and Goddess. This ritual seals your name-taking at a spiritual level—but it does not imply that you cannot take a different circle-name at a later date (see pages 148–151). Some covens like to combine naming with initiation but some witches like to take this name prior to or instead of initiation.

Before the ritual, meditate on a sponsor deity; this could be a god or goddess with whom you have an affinity or a deity of magic. Consider in advance what gifts to ask of each element at your naming. The "subject" in this ritual refers to the person taking a circle-name.

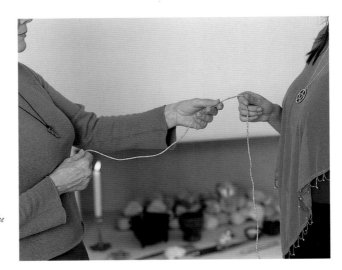

Circle-name ceremonies are a formal means by which you draw the attention of the God or Goddess to your chosen spiritual identity.

RITUAL

You will need

- Initiation incense
- Large feather in the Air quarter
- Salt in Earth quarter
- Water in Water quarter
- Tea-light in Fire quarter
- Silver/gray cord in Spirit

Performing the ritual

1 Cast a circle.

2 Four officers welcome the elements as they normally would for an esbat.

Subject walks to the center and declares: "In this space between the worlds I take a name by which I shall be known within the sacred circle and by the elements and the God and Goddess. I take the name [name] and call upon [God or Goddess] to witness and bless this naming."

3 Subject moves deosil to the Air quarter. Air officer says: "By what name will you be known to me?"

Subject responds with chosen name. Air officer says: "What gift do you ask of me at this your naming?" Subject responds appropriately. Air officer responds by wafting incense smoke over subject with the aid of the feather.

4 The subject moves through Fire, Water and Earth, repeating the exchanges above with each officer: Fire officer lights the tealight; Water officer sprinkles the Subject with water and the Earth officer gives her/him salt to taste.

5 Subject comes to the center to stand before Spirit. Spirit officer says: "By what name will you be known to the Goddess?" Subject responds. Spirit officer says: "What gift do you ask of Her at this your naming?" Subject responds. Spirit officer then hands the subject a length of silver/gray cord that should be kept on a permanent altar or other safe place by the subject.

6 Thank the elements and close the circle.

Severing ceremony

To handfast with another is to make a commitment within sacred space which resonates at a spiritual and emotional level. It is important, therefore, if a decision is made to separate, that you go into sacred space to sever that bond.

Although endings can be painful, it is to be hoped that you can treat each other with the respect that you promised at your handfasting, and sort out your affairs in a civilized manner. It is helpful to perform this ceremony together, whether alone or with witnesses. If this is not possible, the ritual can be adjusted to perform it alone. The outline that follows assumes that you are both present and have friends on hand to perform the offices required, including an Advocate to help you through the ceremony.

RITUAL

You will need
- Length of black cord long enough to go around both wrists, with about 12 inches (30 cm) to spare
- Sharp athame
- Black candle
- Salt dispenser

Performing the ritual

1 Cast the circle.

2 Officers welcome the elements as they normally would for an esbat. The Advocate says: "We are here because [name 1] and [name 2] wish to part in honor and before the God and Goddess who blessed their joining together. [name 1] Do you agree that this is why you are here?" Name 1 responds: "Yes." The

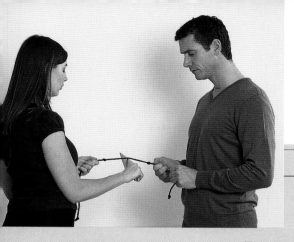

Severing ceremonies are part of the process of separation.

Advocate repeats the request to name 2 who should give assent.

3 Advocate lights the black candle at center circle, saying: "I invoke Saturn, Old One, Wise One, to witness the parting of [name 1] and [name 2]. May the Goddess who joined them now witness the severing of the bond and bless each of them as they journey their separate paths."

4 The Advocate ties or asks the partners to tie the ends of the black cord around the wrist of the hand that was joined with that of their partner at the handfasting, leaving about 12 inches (30 cm) of cord stretched between them tightly.

5 Name 1 pours a line of salt on the floor between the partners, saying: "Thus we are parted." Name 2 takes the athame and severs the cord stretched between them, saying: "Thus we are parted."

6 The Advocate says: "You have parted with honor; let the healing begin." The black cord bracelets should be removed after the ritual and buried deep in Earth away from home.

Self-blessing ritual

There are times after great change, after trauma or when we are suffering from self-doubt when we need spiritual sustenance. It is believed that this blessing ritual is based on a very ancient tradition; the salt represents the security and sanctuary of Earth and the candle flame represents moving from the fog of fear into the light of the Goddess's protection. The ritual below is designed specifically for solo work. The Dark Moon is the best time for self-blessing. However, as this ritual is only ever worked in times of need, it is likely that this, rather than the Moon phase, will be your priority. You should perform this ritual sky-clad—naked.

A self-blessing should be performed only in need.

RItUAL

You will need
- White candle
- Salt
- Anointing oil (see pages 342–343) or if working in haste, a little pure olive oil

Peforming the ritual

1 Cast a circle.

2 Welcome in the element of Air, saying: "In the east the element of Air, I call you into

the circle. Mighty Ones protect me."
Repeat this, moving deosil around
the circle, calling in Fire, Water, and
Earth in turn.

3 At the center, welcome Spirit,
saying: "In the center, at the margins
and in all the spaces in between,
element of Spirit guide and protect
me." Sprinkle the salt on the floor in
front of you and step onto it saying:
"Earth beneath my feet offer me
sanctuary from the cares of the
world." Light the white candle and
step back from it.

Take the oil and anoint your feet,
knees, sex, breast, lips, saying at the
appropriate time:

*Blessed be my feet that they
  may walk the sacred path
Blessed be my knees that they
  may never kneel in fear
Blessed be my womb/phallus
  without which we would
  not be*

*Blessed be my breast and the
  strong heart within
Blessed be my lips that they
  may speak Her will*

4 Step into the light of the candle,
saying:

*I step into the light of the
  Goddess, into Her arms and
  into Her protection
Her light is my shield and Her
  embrace my armor
She walks with me in my
  footsteps
She is above and below me
To the East and the West of me
Before and behind me
Within and around me*

5 Close your eyes and remain in the
warmth and light of the candle for as
long as your need directs you.

ʄuneral ceremony

The last rite of passage is that from life into death and, although Wiccan beliefs vary, there are some traditions associated with the leaving of life. Rhiannon, Celtic goddess of horses and natural justice, is seen as the deity who midwifes the dying into the other side of death. The reference to the "sweet birds of Rhiannon" in the ritual below alludes to the belief that, at her command, birdsong guides the spirit of the dead to make their passage easier.

Funerals serve a different purpose from that of a memorial service. The ritual here is along the lines of a "commital;" it focuses on our duty to care for the body and spirit of the dead. At a pagan funeral it is not unusual to have the body of the deceased on full view, either dressed ceremonially or in a shroud, and placed on a pallet.

*A funeral marks
the transition
from life into
death and beyond.*

RITUAL

You will need

- Bunches of rosemary, for remembrance, to place on the body at the appropriate moment

Performing the ritual

1 Cast a circle with the body of the dead one at the center.

2 Officer for Air says: "In the east, I welcome the element of Air and ask that our memories of [name of dead person] stay true and do not alter with the passing of time." Officer for Fire says: "In the south, I welcome the element of Fire and ask that we remember her/him as she/he was in life and keep that in our hearts."

3 Officer for Water says: "In the west, I welcome the element of Water and ask that the love that she/he brought to our lives stays with us for ever." Officer for Earth says: "In the north, I welcome the element of Earth and ask that

her/his presence among us, and what she/he left behind, is honored in death as it was in life."

4 Officer for Spirit says: "[Name], we send you on your journey from this world with our memories, with our cherished thoughts, with our love and with our hands."

5 Mourners may offer brief readings, songs or poems before taking a bunch of rosemary to place on the body.

6 Officer for Spirit says: "[Name], may the sweet birds of Rhiannon guide you on your journey, may your spirit fly as straight as an arrow to the heart of the Sun, may your spirit be still and know rest. Blessed Be."

7 The body should be lifted on a pallet by several mourners of similar height and carried to the place where it is to be burned or buried.

Glossary

Air One of the five elements. In sacred space, the Air Quarter is often decorated in yellow, with wind-chimes, feathers, carved birds, airborne seeds, scented herbs such as lavender or mint, and wands. It may include symbols or depictions of deities we associate with Air: Athena, goddess of wisdom; or Hermes (Mercury), god of swiftness and communication.

Alexandrian This form of Wicca developed out of the Gardnerian system in the 1960s and is named for Alex Sanders, who with his partner Maxine developed a tradition that incorporated elements of Judeo-Christian sources, as well as aspects of the Greek and Egyptian mysteries and Celtic traditions. Alexandrians honor the triple Goddess in all her aspects and dual God.

Altar A focal point for sacred and magical activity within the circle. Traditionally set up in the north, but sometimes placed at the center, the place of Spirit, the altar holds the tools and ingredients of ritual.

Ankh An ancient Egyptian symbol associated with Isis, the All-Mother and goddess of magic and healing. The loop is a yonic—female sexual—symbol, while the downward strut is phallic. In conjunction these bring forth life and so the ankh is seen as the key to fertility, rebirth, and eternal life.

Avalon The Isle of Apples (fruit of the Celtic otherworld).

Balefire A fire set for magical or ritual purposes.

Beltane Celtic fire festival. Celebrated on May I in the northern hemisphere and October 31 in the southern.

Celtic knot A knot-work design formed from a single unbroken thread. It signifies the nature of eternity and the Universe.

Celtic Tree Alphabet The Celts had such a strong affinity with trees that they invented a tree alphabet, the *Beth-Luis-Nion*, sometimes *Beth-Luis-Fearn*. All the letters are related to a shrub or tree, and those born in the lunar month relating to that tree are said to bear some of its qualities, rather like the zodiac signs in astrology.

Chalice The chalice is associated with Water and is traditionally given to a witch, as it represents the element of love. This contains the wine or juice that is passed around the circle before the end of a ritual and can be used in spell-work.

Circle The circle represents a universal and spiritually relevant paradox—it is a shape without beginning and without end. In Wicca, we do most of our ritual and spell-work within a circle, cast by a witch in order to define the boundaries of the place where we come face to face with our deities, where we work magic, and enter altered states of consciousness.

Coven It is usual for covens to meet for circle-work at least once a month for esbats. Larger covens may also make separate arrangements to accommodate circle-work outside of the main group as training sessions for newcomers. It is common for covens to be called together to do adhoc healing work or when there is a crisis or an emergency involving a group member. Some old-fashioned covens still have a high priest or priestess, though many now pass this office around the more experienced members of the group or dispense with it altogether if the group is organized in a non-hierarchical fashion.

Crone A post-menstrual women.

Cunning-man A man who serves a community and is knowledgeable in the ways of nature, herbal magic, and traditional healing.

Dark moon When the Moon is entirely covered by Earth's shadow.

Deosil Sunwise (clockwise).

Druid Close Celtic pagan relatives of witches. They revere nature as divine, celebrate, generally, the four major solar festivals, and honor a God or Goddess. They sometimes organize along initiatory and hierarchical lines, but not always. Like witches, Druids are male or female.

Earth One of the five elements. The Earth is found in the rocks, mountains, valleys and underground caverns. In sacred space, the Earth quarter is usually decorated in green, and contains living plants, wood, crystals and stones, fallen branches and images of forest creatures, earthy herbs, gums and oils such as patchouli, cypress, yew or mandrake, and a pentacle. The Earth quarter may include images of appropriate deities such as Demeter, the harvest goddess or the Green Man.

Eight-spoked wheel This is a symbol of the sacred year, each spoke representing one of the seasonal Sabbats. It sometimes symbolizes the Wheel of Fortuna, goddess of chance and fate in the Roman pantheon.

Elements The five sacred elements of which the Universe is composed: Air, Fire, Water, Earth, and Spirit.

Eostre Fertility goddess associated with the spring equinox.

Equinox The spring and autumn equinoxes are the two days of perfect balance between the hours of daylight and darkness. In the northern hemisphere the spring equinox falls on March 21 or 22 and the autumn equinox on September 21 or 22. In the southern hemisphere the equinoxes are reversed.

Esbat Esbats are traditionally Full-Moon circles. Covens generally adhere to this, though some like to celebrate different phases of the Moon together occasionally. The main purpose of group esbats is to celebrate and honor the deities, to work toward spiritual development, to develop magical and ritual skills, and to raise energy together to cast spells.

Eye of Horus A protection against evil and a symbol of seeing or wisdom. Horus is a god of health and regeneration, and so his symbol carries some significance for contemporary pagans.

Fire One of the five elements. Fire is seen in the warmth of the Sun and the temperature needed to keep all things in balance. In sacred space, the Fire Quarter is often decorated in red, with candles, lamps, carved dragons or salamanders, flowers and associated herbs, spices and gums such as frankincense, cinnamon, cactus or coriander, and athames (witches' knives) or swords. It may include symbols or images of deities associated with Fire: Brighid, Celtic fire goddess or Belenos, god of the Sun.

Gaia The primal Earth-mother who gave birth pathenogenically (without insemination) to the Waters, the Sky, and the Mountains. The interconnected biosystem that links all beings and elements on the planet—as a whole being—is called Gaia.

Gardnerian Named for Gerald Gardner, this tradition enfolds elements of ancient traditions and because of its local origins, the folklore and customs of English paganism.

Green Man The consort of the Goddess and ancient spirit of the Greenwood. In Wicca the Green Man is seen both as an aspect of the god and as a champion of environmentalism.

Hag The crone aspect of the Goddess who midwives us with great compassion, from life to death.

Handfasting A marriage ceremony. Ceremonies commonly include vows that hold for either a year and a day or for as long as love lasts. This is in recognition that people continue changing after they fall in love, and that a vow to stay together for eternity may not reflect this.

Hecate Dark goddess of magic—weaver of wisdom and guardian at the crossroads.

Hedgewitch Solo workers are sometimes called Hedgewitches, though strictly speaking, Hedgewitchery is the work of a Wise-Woman or Cunning-Man serving a community, knowledgeable in the ways of nature, herbal magic, and traditional healing.

Hereditary In Wicca, a Hereditary is a witch who has inherited craft knowledge through their own family, or initiation into a hereditary group.

Imbolc Celtic fire festival. Celebrated on February 1/2 in the northern hemisphere and August 1/2 in the southern.

Initiation An act of commitment to the Goddess—the patron of initiation—signaling to the great web that connects all things that you stand before the deities to dedicate yourself to the ways of the wise.

Initiation cord Cords that are the exact height, head circumference, and distance around the heart of an initiate.

John Barleycorn The caring father aspect of the god. He weds the pregnant Goddess at Beltane and is cut down at Lughnasadh as the harvest to feed the people.

Labyrinth A labyrinth depicts the journey from birth, through life, to death and rebirth, and is found on many of the ancient monuments of the world.

Law of Threefold Return The belief that whatever you send out is returned to you threefold.

Litha The summer solstice. Celebrated on June 21/22 in the northern hemisphere and December 21/22 in the southern.

Lughnasadh Celtic fire festival. Celebrated on August 1/2 in the northern hemisphere and February 1/2 in the southern.

Maze Mazes are symbols of the left-brain functions, of rationality, and reason.

Modron The autumn equinox. Celebrated on September 21/22 in the northern hemisphere and March 21/22 in the southern.

Moon The Moon is our closest celestial neighbor. It produces the tides on the waters of Earth and influences the reproductive cycles of some animals. The full cycle of the Moon through its phases from new (or dark) Moon, first quarter, half, full, last quarter, and back to new or dark again is 29.5 days.

Mother charge A recitation by a priestess at esbats.

New Moon When the Moon is entirely covered by Earth's shadow.

Ostara The spring equinox. Celebrated on March 21/22 in the northern hemisphere and September 21/22 in the southern.

Pentacle A five-pointed star within a circle. A pentacle signifies variously the circle of the Earth or the unified nature of the Universe. The five points pertain to the five sacred elements Air, Fire, Water, Earth, and Spirit.

Pentagram A five-pointed star. This is one of the most commonly sported symbols in Wicca.

Polytheistic A religion that does not adhere to just one god or goddess.

Qabalah Derived from ancient Jewish mysticism, it is a body of occult knowledge that is supposed to contain the secrets of the Universe.

Rede A Middle English word derived from Old English and Old High German, is thought to mean "advice." The Wiccan Rede is a guide to making decisions about how we act.

Runes The letters of an ancient Germanic alphabet developed over the last two millennia to form 24 symbols. The characters are formed from straight lines, reflecting their early origins when they were carved into stone or wood. Runes also carried meaning beyond their written or phonetic usage; they embodied esoteric knowledge and power and were used for divination and magic.

Sabbat Seasonal festivals. There are eight seasonal festivals in the Wiccan year—Samhain, Yule, Imbolc, Ostara, Beltane, Litha, Lughnasadh, and Modron.

Sacred circle A circle cast by a witch in order to define the boundaries of the place where we come face to face with our deities, where we work magic, and enter altered states of consciousness. This space is sacred because it is dedicated to the God and Goddess and their work. The boundaries of the circle are protected by the elements and deities we call in and honor.

Samhain Celtic fire festival. Celebrated on the last day of October in the northern hemisphere and the first day of May in the southern.

Saex-Wicca This was formulated by Raymond Buckland, who is also accredited with introducing Wicca to the US. Saex-Wicca is based on the Gardnerian framework, but draws in aspects of English Saxon and Scots Pictish traditions.

Scrying The technique of focusing on a magical tool such as a mirror, a crystal ball, or flame in order to receive images and thoughts that reveal a truth or a message concerning a particular situation.

Sephiroth Spheres on the Tree of Life. Each sphere represents an aspect of life and spiritual enlightenment, and each has planetary and angelic correspondences.

Six-pointed star This six-pointed star unites the symbols of the four physical elements and its symmetry visibly demonstrates the Hermetic principle, "As above, So below." In Wicca it is a symbol of Hermetic significance, as well as the conjunction of the elements. It is also known as the Star of David and a symbol of the Jewish faith.

Solitary Witches who practice on their own.

Solstice The winter and summer solstices are the shortest and longest days of the year. In the northern hemisphere the shortest day at the winter solstice usually falls on December 21 or 22, the longest day at the summer solstice on June 21 or 22. In the southern hemisphere the solstices are reversed.

Spiral The spiral denotes the microcosmic and macrocosmic order of the Universe. Like the web, it is a symbol of the element of Spirit.

Spirit The fifth element that causes the first four elements to conjoin in particular proportions and forms to produce life and the Universe as we experience it. Spirit is the sacred weaver of the elements and as "the connection" is, along with the other four, an equal cause and part of the Universe. It is also the great web of life that joins all beings to each other. In sacred space, Spirit is set in the center of the ritual space. It is decorated in purple or white and may include spider and web symbols and totems denoting divine "magical" patrons such as Hecate or Changing Woman.

Summerlands In Celtic mythology, this is the land of the ever-young, where healing waters flow and the old, the sick, and those who have suffered are restored. Some witches speak of those who have died as having "passed over to the Summerlands."

Tarot A Tarot deck consist of 72 cards, all of which symbolize arcane aspects of events, character, and influences in our lives. There are also four suits of cards: cups, coins, blades, and rods, which correspond with the first four sacred elements in Wicca—cups with Water, coins with Earth, blades with Air, and rods with Fire.

Tree of Life The Tree of Life is based on the ancient system of the Qabalah, and shows a structure of archetypal spheres organized in a geometric pattern which simplify the complex nature of reality.

Triskele A three-legged symbol of Celtic art that depicts the power of three—Earth, Water, and Fire.

Visualization The ability to hold in your mind's eye, aspects of your inner, spiritual landscape or to imagine the intended outcome of a spell. An important part of self-development, spell-work and ritual.

Waning moon The shrinking cycle of the Moon.

Water One of the five elements. Water is in the rains that nourish the crops and vegetation, in the streams, rivers, seas, and oceans. In sacred space, the Water quarter is often decorated in blue, with glass pebbles, depictions of sea-creatures, watery herbs and flowers such as roses, hyacinths, myrtle, and lovage, and a chalice. It may include symbols or images of Water-associated deities such as: Rhiannon, Welsh goddess of rebirth, or Yemana, Santeria goddess of the sea.

Waxing moon The growing cycle of the Moon.

Web A network of existence through which all beings are linked. The web symbolizes sacred connection, which we also understand variously as Spirit and/or the God and Goddess.

Wiccan Rede A guide to making decisions about how we act.

Widdershins Anti-sunwise (anti-clockwise).

Wise Witches call themselves Wicca ("wise" in Anglo-Saxon).

Wise-woman A woman who serves a community and is knowledgeable in the ways of nature, herbal magic, and traditional healing.

Yule The winter solstice. Celebrated on December 21/22 in the northern hemisphere and June 21/22 in the southern.

Index

Acknowledgments

Special Photography: © Octopus Publishing Group Limited/Russell Sadur

Other Photography: Alamy/Nigel Hicks 68-69; /Ronald Weir 38-39. **Bridgeman Art Library, London/New York**/www.bridgeman.co.uk/Bibliotheque Nationale, Paris, France 358; /Freja Seeking Her Husband, 1852 (oil on canvas), Blommer, Nils (1816–53)/Nationalmuseum, Stockholm, Sweden 125; /Lambeth Palace Library, London, UK 307; /Manchester Art Gallery, UK 363; /National Museum of Iceland, Reykjavik, Iceland 126; /Private collection, The Stapleton Collection 302; /Royal Library, Copenhagen, Denmark 129. **Collections**/Robert Pilgrim 360; /Brian Shuel 66. **Corbis UK Ltd**/58, 196; /Alinari Archives 106; /Bettmann 300; /Jim Craigmyle 178; /Gianni Dagli 117; /Macduff Everton 350-351; /Freelance Consulting Services Pty Ltd 190-191; /Greenhalf Photography 63; /Jason Hawkes 175; /Angelo Hornak 130; /Archivo Iconografico 311; /Mimmo Jodice 112; /Araldo de Luca 109; /David Muench 192; /Kevin Schafer 46-47; /Ted Spiegel 36; /Sandro Vannini 105; /Adam Woolfitt 189; /Roger Wood 118. **Mary Evans Picture Library** 122. **Getty Images** 21, 92-93, 168, 320, 369; /Adastra 209; /Richard Ashworth 100; /Ken Biggs 152; /Brand X Pictures 148-149; /Thomas Broad 22; /Comstock Images 30; /Nick Dolding 244; /Georgette Douwma 167; /Robert Everts 17; /Fischer 64; /Ken Gillham 367; /Peter Gridley 104; /A. Hansen 9; /Robert Harding 144; /Tom Murphy 142; /Fergus O'Brian 172; /Photodisc Green 241; /Planet Earth/Mike Coltman 164; /Jurgen Reisch 31; /David Sacks 34, 283; /Miquel S. Salmeron 19; /Tom Schierlitz 313; /Steve Taylor 353; /Adrian Weinbrecht 138; /Frank Whitney 67. **Octopus Publishing Group Limited** 16, 26, 33, 61, 70, 81, 82, 197, 250, 282, 284, 286, 290, 291, 292, 299, 324, 348; /Colin Bowling 328 top right, 329 bottom right, 330, 332, 336, 338; /Michael Boys 98-99, 326; /Nick Carman 72; /Jerry Harpur 51, 334; /Mike Hemsley 83, 204, 205, 217, 240, 345; /Neil Holmes 327; /Sandra Lane 331; /Sean Myers 32; Ian Parsons 65, 85 bottom, 143, 200, 294, 298, 323; /Peter Pugh-Cook 275; /Guy Ryecart 88; /Roger Stowell 325, 329 top left, 340, 341; /Mark Winwood 194; /George Wright 62, 328 bottom left, 333. **Nasa** 20, 208. **Rubberball** 4-5, 79.

With thanks to Mystics & Magic (www.mysticsandmagic.co.uk) for props borrowed on shoot.

Executive Editor Brenda Rosen

Managing Editor Clare Churly

Executive Art Editor Sally Bond

Designer Julie Francis

Picture Library Manager Jennifer Veall

Production Manager Louise Hall